DEVOTIONS FOR Gardeners

DEVOTIONS
~FOR~
Gardeners

Jean Shaw

ZondervanPublishingHouse
Grand Rapids, Michigan

A Division of HarperCollins*Publishers*

Devotions for Gardeners
Copyright © 1994 by Jean Shaw

Shaw, Jean, 1929–
        Devotions for gardeners / by Jean Shaw.
                p.   cm.
        ISBN 0-310-37510-X
        1. Gardeners—Prayer-books and devotions—English. 2.
Gardens—Religious aspects—Christianity—Meditations. I. Title.
BV4596.G36S53 1993
242--dc20   93-39073

                                                      CIP.

All Scripture quotations, unless otherwise noted, are taken from the Holy Bible: New International Version (North American Edition). Copyright © 1973, 1978, 1984, by the International Bible Society. Used by permission of Zondervan Bible Publishers.

Requests for information should be addressed to:

Zondervan Publishing House
5300 Patterson Avenue S.E.
Grand Rapids, Michigan 49530

Edited by Anne Severance
Interior design by Sharon Wright
Cover design by Sharon Wright

Printed in the United States of America

93   94   95   96   97   98   /❖ DC/ 10   9   8   7   6   5   4   3   2   1

This edition is printed on acid-free paper and meets the American National Standards Institute Z39.48 standard.

Contents

FOR MY BROTHER MARC

*"How deeply seated
in the human heart
is the liking for gardens
and gardening."*

— *ALEXANDER SMITH*

In the Beginning . . .

*The land produced vegetation: plants bearing
seed according to their kinds and trees bearing
fruit with seed in it according to their kinds. And
God saw that it was good.*

—GENESIS 1:12

The Bible begins with a garden. Within this limited industry and location, God reveals his many attributes. By the end of the first chapter of Genesis, we have learned that God is the wise and powerful Creator and Sustainer of all things.

In chapter 2, we read of God's love for mankind, how he breathed into Adam's nostrils his very own breath and then put us in families to love and care for each other. In chapter 3, we see God's judgment, coupled with his incomparable mercy. In the garden God promises the coming of his Son and his eventual victory over Satan, epitomized by the wily serpent.

The events that occurred in the Garden of Eden provide the bedrock of our Christian faith. As we ponder the fall of man, it is easy to miss some details about the garden itself. We note that no plants had sprung up voluntarily. Every plant and tree was an original, designed by God himself, and from these basic plants come all the amazing hybrids we enjoy today. Since the Creation, no one has invented a "new" plant!

The Bible states that God had sent no rain on the earth; the garden was kept moist by underground streams that watered the whole surface of the earth. This is a common form of irrigation in many parts of our country, including eastern Idaho, where a network of canals carries water from the Snake River. By raising the metal plate that covers a culvert, the farmer can flood his fields.

Having set the plants in the ground and watered them, God then put Adam in the Garden of Eden to work it and to take care of it. This was done before the curse of thorns and thistles made gardening "painful toil." Food-producing plants have always needed some kind of tending.

There is no place for arrogance in a garden. Both our materials and our methods have as their origin the wisdom and creativity of God.

HEARTICULTURE: A red ribbon for our rutabagas can bring forth a prideful attitude. The proud gardener may fail to remember the miracle of growth from the tiny seed. As you tend your plants today, reflect on their Source.

HORTICULTURE: Seeds from hybrid flowers and vegetables will usually not breed true the following year. Purchase fresh seeds of new varieties.

Thorns and Thistles

Cursed is the ground because of you; through
painful toil you will eat of it all the days of your
life. It will produce thorns and thistles for you,
and you will eat the plants of the field.
                      —GENESIS 3:17–18

It has been said that weeds are plants whose virtues have not been discovered. But with the modern pharmacy, stocked with its chemical wonders, now replacing the town herbalist, the medicinal and household value of many weeds extolled in earlier times often escapes us. And it's really tough to find the merits of a "plant" that grows best where it is not wanted!

As we attack another clump of purslane, the thought runs through our minds that weeds "are the result of the fall." Like houseflies. Except that weeds are only mentioned once in the Bible, and that's in the sense of seaweed (Jonah 2:5). The plant pests in Bible lands were thorns and thistles—the brier and brambles type—rather than the small spikeless varieties which harass today's gardeners.

Pulling out crabgrass that has gone astray is one thing. Digging out a thistle is quite another. Every bit of root must be removed or another thistle will pop up, more resistant than ever. As for thorns, a suit of armor is not protection enough against them! A friend of mine accepted a job, with good pay, of removing a pyrocantha hedge that ran along the entire side of a house. He came home every night, literally bloody and beaten.

Life has its weeds, those pesky annoyances that slow us down and keep us from quickly reaching our goal. Their cause may have nothing to do with us at all. God's curse concerns the thorns and thistles, those deep-rooted sins that must be hacked down and dug out completely, using every spiritual tool at our disposal.

God knows the difference between a weed and a thistle. So should we.

HEARTICULTURE: We can become so obsessed with the weeds in our lives that we ignore the thorns and thistles. For example, we are limited in what we can do about interruptive telephone calls. These are weeds. But choosing to respond with irritation is a thistle that demands intensive eradication.

HORTICULTURE: Learn to identify weeds as either annuals or perennials. Annuals respond to regular hoeing. Perennials must be removed carefully, roots and all, or they will be that much more resistant next year. One of the best ways to control weeds is the liberal use of mulch or black plastic, which shuts out sunlight and stops their growth.

No More Tomatoes, Please!

In the desert the whole community grumbled against Moses and Aaron. The Israelites said to them, "If only we had died by the LORD's hand in Egypt! There we sat around pots of meat and ate all the food we wanted, but you have brought us out into this desert to starve this entire assembly to death."

—EXODUS 16:2–3

Well, yes, the meat was free—and they had all they wanted. But the hidden cost of this "free" food was slavery. There are millions of people in formerly communist countries who decided that government-supplied food was not worth that price. Even so, as food supplies adjust to a new kind of economy, there are those who want to return to security with bondage.

In my home canning phase, I would spend nine months yearning for a genuine home-grown tomato. Oh, the deliciousness of that very first one, picked off the vine and eaten right on the spot! How good the first platter of beefsteaks, sprinkled with oil and vinegar and a few snips of oregano. How tasty the tomatoes that were broiled, stewed, baked, or tucked with lettuce and bacon between two slices of bread.

Then came the hours of canning and the indescribable thrill of seeing all fifty-six quarts lined up on the shelves. But, oh, the day after the canner was stored for the winter, and a church friend dropped by with a big bag of her surplus tomatoes! I was sick of tomatoes! I didn't even want to look at a *picture* of a tomato!

We do like to choose our blessings. If God would only space our good times evenly through life, we would never complain. Or would we? Human beings have very short memories. We are also notoriously hard to please. We remember our pots of meat, but forget how hard we worked to make bricks from straw.

Like the Israelites in the desert, obsessed with self-pity, we wail. We rebel. We demand an alternative. And because we will learn thankfulness in no other way, God gives us exactly what we want until we've had enough of that, too, and learn to trust him to give us what is best for us.

HEARTICULTURE: Can you honestly say that you have peace in your present situation? Do you crave meat, like the Israelites did? If God chose to send you some, as he sent quails to his people in the desert, how much would be enough?

ɣ HORTICULTURE: There are hundreds of varieties of tomatoes, but basically two types—determinate and indeterminate. Determinate tomatoes, such as Big Early, Better Boy, Big Girl, and Beefmaster, grow to a certain size and produce a set amount of fruit. These are good for canning, since there is a large crop to process all at once. Indeterminate tomatoes, such as Fireball, Celebrity, President, and Marglobe, have no limits, ripen throughout the summer, and are best suited for table use.

Remember That Wonderful Melon?

*The rabble with them began to crave other food,
and again the Israelites started wailing and said,
"If only we had meat to eat! We remember the
fish we ate in Egypt at no cost—also the cucumbers, melons, leeks, onions and garlic. But now
we have lost our appetite; we never see anything
but this manna!"*

—NUMBERS 11:4–6

Somebody spit a watermelon seed into the flower bed that runs along the edge of our patio, and the following summer a watermelon plant sprang up, right in the middle of the impatiens and the ageratum. We just couldn't bring ourselves to pull it out. Growing a watermelon in such an odd place was too much of a challenge!

We positioned the vine along the brick border and watched it circle the bed to a length of twenty feet. It produced two huge, delicious watermelons. Then we invited a group of people over to eat it and spit their seeds into the garden. Not one seed sprouted.

Every vegetable gardener has the memory of at least one special harvest. The first tomato of the summer. The year everything was right for potatoes. We remember our "cucumbers, melons, leeks, onions and garlic," and wish we could go back to those good old days.

Wistful memories are one thing. Complaining because we do not have something we once had is quite another. Grumbling is really saying that God is insufficient. When everything goes wrong, we, too, may be tempted to blame him. But God told the Israelites, and he tells us, that complaining is the same thing as rejecting him. For the Israelites, this terrible sin brought down harsh punishment—first, in a surfeit of quail meat until everyone was sick of it; then, in a severe plague.

In Philippians 2:14, Christians are told specifically to do everything "without complaining or arguing." Each of us has a melon or two we unrealistically hold up as the standard, and against which we compare everything else. Were we to be honest, we would have to admit that what we are remembering wasn't quite as wonderful as we think it was, and that its counterpart today isn't quite as bad.

HEARTICULTURE: Is there some experience in your past that you use as the standard for what happens to you today? Read Isaiah 43:18–19.

HORTICULTURE: Melons need eighty to one hundred days to reach maturity. If your season is shorter, either start your plants indoors three to four weeks before the average last frost, or choose early varieties adapted to cooler conditions. Just remember that the fruits will be smaller.

No More Manna!

*The manna was like coriander seed and looked
like resin. The people went around gathering it,
and then ground it in a handmill or crushed it in
a mortar. They cooked it in a pot or made it into
cakes. And it tasted like something made with
olive oil. When the dew settled on the camp at
night, the manna also came down.*

—*Numbers 11:7–9*

Versatile stuff, that manna. It had other virtues,
too. It was nutritionally balanced and sustained
the Israelites for forty years. Besides that, God was gracious
to give manna the flavors of popular foods—coriander and
olive oil. Coriander was a tangy herb with medicinal prop-
erties and was prized as a seasoning for food.

The real identity of manna is pure speculation.
Some scholars believe it was the honey-like substance produced by some insects. This substance may be picked up
from the ground in the early morning, but only for a few
weeks each year. Nothing but a miracle, however, can
explain the consistency of the supply of manna, or the fact
that it was withheld every seventh day.

Before we criticize the Israelites for grumbling
about what appears to be the ideal solution to their food
problem, let us ask ourselves if we would like to eat the
same thing every day for forty years, no matter how many
ways it was served! Forty *days* of zucchini would be a test!

Manna was God's visual aid to teach his people to
look beyond their stomachs to see their spiritual needs.

"Man does not live on bread alone," God told them, "but on every word that comes from the mouth of the LORD" (Deut. 8:3). There are more important activities than eating. Jesus referred to himself as the Bread of Life. "He who comes to me will never go hungry, and he who believes in me will never be thirsty" (John 6:35).

As we stand in our vegetable garden, glorying in the results of our labors, it is very easy to be consumed with pride. We may forget that life is much more than the production of broccoli and sweet corn. Jesus asks us to feed on him so that we may have eternal life.

HEARTICULTURE: We are reminded that, for all its life-sustaining qualities, manna did not prevent death. Ultimately, all living creatures must die. Only Jesus offers the bread that will enable us to live forever. To eat this bread means to believe in him and to know him so thoroughly, through the reading of his Word, that his nature becomes ours.

HORTICULTURE: How big should a vegetable garden be? One guide says a plot 50' x 50' will feed a family of four—but you'd better plan to use a tractor! Current gardening practices take into account today's smaller yards, reluctance to purchase power machinery, and the limited time people have to spend for gardening. Vegetables can be grown in containers, trained along fences, or mixed with flowers—just use your imagination. Nor is it necessary to grow multiples of everything. One cucumber vine, planted in one cubic foot of soil, if fed once every two weeks with a liquid plant food, will produce enough cucumbers to keep that family of four quite content.

Please, Have Some Zucchini

*If you enter your neighbor's vineyard, you may
eat all the grapes you want, but do not put any
in your basket. If you enter your neighbor's
grainfield, you may pick kernels with your
hands, but you must not put a sickle to his standing grain.*

—DEUTERONOMY 23:24–25

When Rosie came for lunch yesterday, she remarked that summer squash, which she loves, isn't available in the stores anymore. "Let's go out to the garden," I said. "I grow summer squash, and there should be some ready for picking." Happily there was plenty, and Rosie went home with a bagful, plus a tender zucchini that just happened to catch my eye.

In biblical times, the idea of sharing one's produce was a law, not an option. The law carried four implications. First, to share something indicates there is something to share! God promised the Israelites an abundant harvest when they settled in Canaan. Secondly, the pronoun *you* refers to another Israelite—a traveler, perhaps, or a poor person. There are many passages in the Scriptures directing us to care for those, particularly in our own fellowship, who are in temporary or continuing need. The book of Ruth emphasized the law of leaving some grain for the poor to harvest. We are not to hoard our bounty, as the man who built bigger barns found out (Luke 12:16–21)!

Third, this law puts into perspective the idea of sharing our property. I would not be happy to see someone stride into my garden without permission and fill up a bushel basket with vegetables. But if someone is so hungry he needs a tomato or two, I am not to make a big fuss over it. There is much we can afford to lose without any harm to ourselves.

Finally, there is the matter of basic hospitality, of being gracious. What I grow in my garden is already a gift from God. When I share, I perpetuate God's blessings in remembrance of the ultimate gift of his Son.

There is more to picking summer squash than we think!

HEARTICULTURE: A priority of the early church was care of orphans, widows, and the poor. People gladly shared their possessions. Special offerings were taken to help others in a time of famine or other need, and deacons were appointed to oversee the daily distribution of food. Does your church demonstrate this same concern?

HORTICULTURE: Community gardens exist in most metropolitan areas. Gifts of seeds and vegetable plants are usually greatly appreciated. Check with the mayor's office or Cooperative Extension Service in your city or region for further information.

Water Deeply

> *He [whose delight is in the law of the LORD] is like a tree planted by streams of water, which yields its fruit in season and whose leaf does not wither. Whatever he does prospers.*
>
> —PSALM 1:3

During one unusually hot October, our cherry tree blossomed, but without the cold nights and warm days of spring, the tree did not produce cherries. Nor did these same branches blossom or bear fruit the following spring. Confused by abnormal growing conditions, the tree did not "yield its fruit in its season."

This psalm does not describe the person who dutifully reads the Bible every day or even the Bible student who diligently searches the Scriptures, hoping to find eternal life. (Jesus talked about this person in John 5:39.) This psalm describes the person who *delights* in the law of the Lord, one who finds uncommon pleasure, even ecstasy, in the activity.

This delight does not come from merely reading the law of the Lord. This great elation results from *doing* what the law says. Here is a believer who is firmly planted, fixed in place, deeply rooted, secure. She is not sitting in a tub on castors, but by a stream of life-giving water—God's refreshing Spirit. As the believer draws deeply from this stream, she remains green and fruitful. She prospers.

But why does the psalmist include the phrase "in season"? He is telling us that the person who delights in

God's law will produce fruit in both adversity and prosperity—whatever the season. Unlike our cherry tree, which can bear cherries only under ideal conditions at one stated time, the godly person bears fruit regardless of circumstances.

HEARTICULTURE: To keep from withering, a tree must send its roots down to the constantly moist depths of the earth. If we are to weather life's dry times, our delight in God's law must be a continual process. An occasional soaking won't do.

HORTICULTURE: In dry periods, a newly planted fruit tree needs six to eight gallons of water once a week. Frequent, shallow watering will encourage shallow roots. Be sure to water deeply.

Power in a Hailstone

He [God] parted the heavens and came down;
dark clouds were under his feet. He mounted the
cherubim and flew; he soared on the wings of the
wind. He made darkness his covering, his canopy
around him—the dark rain clouds of the sky.
Out of the brightness of his presence clouds
advanced, with hailstones and bolts of lightning.
The LORD thundered from heaven; the voice of
the Most High resounded.
                                        —PSALM 18:9–13

The drop in temperature was astounding. We went from swelter to sweater in thirty minutes. Even at noon, it was so dark we had to turn on the lights. We watched from the patio door as hailstones hit the concrete and bounced into the flower bed. Out on the highway, hail piled up three inches deep, causing cars to swerve from lane to lane.

An hour later the sun was shining again, and the only hailstones left were those stored in home freezers. I walked around the yard, surveying the damage. Stems were beaten to the ground. Leaves were in shreds. The tomatoes looked like they had been shot with an air rifle.

But people in the path of the storm suffered a hundred times more than I, with my personal store of favorite plants. Whole fields of corn and grain were destroyed, along with a year's income. Even the usually philosophical farmers were dismayed by their loss.

Why does God act in this way? Although his purposes are often beyond knowing, one reason might be our need to be reminded of his awesome power. Marvels from the chemical industry, multi-purpose mulchers, and hybridized wonders can lead us to believe that technology is the god of horticulture.

Then Elohim, Creator and Sustainer of the universe, exerts his force to bring us to an acknowledgment of his sovereignty. In the midst of our tools and sprays, he reminds us that he alone is God.

HEARTICULTURE: It is never God's purpose to destroy his people, but rather to strengthen their trust in him. This psalm ends with the words, "He shows unfailing kindness to his anointed, to David and his descendants forever." Often, the aftermath of a natural disaster is an outpouring of Christian compassion and help.

HORTICULTURE: It is during pleasant weather that we should be securing vulnerable plants against the possibility of destruction. Stakes, wire cages, and various other kinds of supports need to be set in place early in the growing season. Insert poles or stakes to a depth of one foot and tie the plants loosely.

An Abundance of Tomatoes

You crown the year with your bounty, and your carts overflow with abundance. The grasslands of the desert overflow; the hills are clothed with gladness.

—PSALM 65:11–12

When I think of a cart overflowing with abundance, I think of tomatoes. In August there is no end to this juicy fruit! If the season is favorable, everyone has a big crop, and using up all those tomatoes is a challenge. For the third time in my life, I have given up canning, and this time I really mean it. So what do I do with all the tomatoes I grew just because I like to grow tomatoes? As the mother of quadruplets said, "Lord, help me to endure my blessings!"

There are places in this world where one tomato could prolong a life. Here, in America, we have such an abundance of food we can't use it all. As·I write this, western-grown peaches are being discarded by the side of the road. There are too many to sell, and they are too fragile to ship.

When David wrote this psalm, about 1000 B.C., there was a much closer connection between agriculture and a beneficent God. The farmer did not credit environmental manipulation for a good crop. The cook did not give thanks to a canning company. It was the Lord who sent the rain, whose hand restrained the pestilence.

As we view our garden in its abundance, it is easy to believe that our success is a result of using the right fertilizer and sprays. Or because we had the advantage of hybridized seeds. Or because our new cultivator-mulcher allows us to maintain a larger area.

The source of our blessings remains the same. "You [God] care for the land and water it; you enrich it abundantly. The streams of God are filled with water to provide the people with grain, for so you have ordained it" (v. 9). A cart of tomatoes should immediately remind us of our loving God.

HEARTICULTURE: In England, many churches hold a harvest festival in the autumn. Vegetables are brought to the sanctuary and arranged in attractive displays. Perhaps we should adopt this practice in our churches, to help us remember who really provides our food.

HORTICULTURE: Some tomatoes are ready to harvest as early as fifty-five days after planting. Others may take ninety days. Plan your garden to include early (Early Girl, New Yorker, Spring Giant), midseason (Burpee's VF, Champion, Jet Star), and late-season varieties (Beefsteak, Oxheart, Rutgers) for a continuous harvest.

A Palm Tree in Church

The righteous will flourish like a palm tree, they will grow like a cedar of Lebanon; planted in the house of the LORD, they will flourish in the courts of our God.

—PSALM 92:12–13

Palm trees may grow singly or in groves. Since they need plenty of water, they are often found near lakes, ponds, and lagoons. Their trunks, eighty or more feet tall and crowned with feathery leaves up to nine feet long, offer relief from the sand and heat of the desert. To "flourish like a palm tree" is to be strong.

It is said that the palm tree has as many uses as there are days in the year. Its fruit, dates, are the chief food of countless tribes in northern Africa today. The seeds of the date can be ground or soaked in water for several days and then used as food for camels, sheep, and goats. The kernel of the date is said to have more food value than barley. Palm wood is used as building timber. The leaves are used for mats, baskets, roofs, and fences. To "flourish like a palm tree" is to be useful!

We righteous-in-the-Lord palm trees are to be planted in the house of the Lord. The church is our base. It is not God's intention that we be isolated houseplants, drying out our fronds on some overheated windowsill. My African violets do best when they are nestled together in trays under a grow light.

To flourish, we must send down roots and draw upon the life-sustaining waters of God's Word and God's people. Are you contributing strength and service in a grove of Christians somewhere?

HEARTICULTURE: Tent, temple, church, city. Throughout the Scriptures, we see that God commends communal worship and service. There is nothing wrong with a temporary retreat into solitude, but the emphasis of God's Word has always been on the congregation.

HORTICULTURE: Date palm seeds may be purchased, or you can start a plant from a date secured in the produce department of a grocery store. Sow the seed one-half inch deep in sandy, humusy soil, kept moist in a temperature of about seventy degrees. If a seedling sprouts, it will be ungainly at first, since the babies do not look like their parents. Enjoy the foliage, as you will not get any fruit!

The Cedar Christian

*The righteous will flourish like a palm tree, they
will grow like a cedar of Lebanon; planted in the
house of the LORD, they will flourish in the courts
of our God.*

—PSALM 92:12–13

Of all the trees the ancient Israelites knew, the cedars of Lebanon were the tallest and most noble. Monarch of the evergreen, the cedar was valued for its beauty and great age, but also for its fragrance and the lasting qualities of its wood. Cedar planks were prized in shipbuilding. Both Solomon's temple and his splendid palace were constructed of cedar.

A cedar grows rapidly, with the potential of reaching a height of 120 feet and a diameter of 8 feet. Of the few remaining trees in Lebanon, their ages range from two hundred to one thousand years old.

The ancient Hebrews regarded the towering cedar of Lebanon as the crowning glory of the plant kingdom. To them, it was a symbol of strength, majesty, and beauty. Is that the image of Christianity we cedars present to the world today? Or would the average arboriculturalist regard us as weak and demeaned, and of a decidedly sordid nature?

To flourish is God's promise to the righteous, those who are obedient and humble before him. In recent days, some of the members of Christ's church, particularly some of its leaders, have proven to be far from righteous.

Repentance is essential if we are to be blessed. Like the forest, restoration begins with each individual tree.

HEARTICULTURE: Ezekiel 31 is a graphic comparison of a cedar of Lebanon with the nation of Assyria, a highly favored people whom God cut down and abandoned because of its pride. Egypt is warned that it, too, will suffer God's wrath because it refuses to acknowledge God as its sovereign Lord. Read and reflect on this chapter. Is America in danger of being cut off from God?

HORTICULTURE: Cedar of Lebanon (*cedrus libani stenocoma*) can be grown in the United States down through Zone 6. A cedar should be planted in good soil in a sunny, protected location. Avoid planting in wet or heavy soils. If growing conditions are favorable, the tree can attain a height of forty feet.

A Ripe Old Age

*They [the righteous] will still bear fruit in old
age, they will stay fresh and green, proclaiming,
"The LORD is upright; he is my Rock, and there
is no wickedness in him."*

—*PSALM 92:14–15*

Three things stand out about the old trees of this passage: They are still bearing fruit, they are vitally alive, and they are praising the Lord. No sour apples here!

One of the most exciting characteristics of the church today is its recognition of senior citizens as useful members. A former social worker gives twenty hours a week in family visitation. A retired company executive serves as business manager of his church.

Older men and women with multiple skills, good health, private income, and the desire to work are being called up to the front ranks of ministry. Mission boards have set up special departments to recruit and train older people for work abroad. Here is a retired computer programmer, self-supporting, eager to live in eastern Europe for two years while a new mission work is organized. There is a surgeon able to spend six weeks working in a hospital in Africa.

How does one stay "fresh and green" after sixty? People of that age are often considered to be resistant to change, always hearkening back to "when I was a child" and never having a new idea. We learn from the preceding passages in this psalm that these righteous souls remained youthful and vigorous by proclaiming God's love from morning to night. They sang a lot. They reflected on the Lord's victories.

There is no spiritual retirement for those whose roots draw nourishment from the living water of God's Word.

HEARTICULTURE: If you are not a senior citizen, how do you regard older people? If you are in that category, how do you regard yourself? Read Job 12:12.

HORTICULTURE: The oldest living things on earth are thought to be the Bristlecone pines on the White Mountains in the Inyo National Forest of California. They are estimated to be 4,600 years old.

Seeds of Kindness

Restore our fortunes, O LORD, like streams in the Negev. Those who sow in tears will reap with songs of joy. He who goes out weeping, carrying seed to sow, will return with songs of joy, carrying sheaves with him.

—PSALM 126:4–6

How could anyone weep while sowing seeds? To the gardener, planting time is the happiest time of the year. At last, the gorgeous pictures from the seed catalogs are about to become reality before our very eyes. Or so we hope!

This psalm celebrates the return of God's people from their exile to Babylonia. For years they had suffered, far from the homeland they loved so well. Life had to go on, nonetheless, and the basic tasks of survival had to be performed. In that alien land, however, spring planting didn't hold its usual joy, for it served to remind them of their captivity. For the older people who remembered Canaan, life under Cyrus, benevolent ruler that he was, was a far cry from life in the Promised Land. Still, God keeps his promises, and eventually the exiles returned home.

Often we must minister in the Lord's name in what seems to be a hopeless situation. We sow our seeds of kindness in the midst of pain or sorrow, expecting a poor crop, if any crop at all. "What good can come of this ministry?" we ask.

Let us be encouraged by this song, which reminds us that the seeds we sow and the tears we shed are not lost. Loved ones can come to know the Lord. Church wounds can be healed. A weak marriage can become strong. The day is coming when we shall reap a joyous harvest.

HEARTICULTURE: In times of discouragement, it is helpful to reflect on what God has already accomplished. Praise him for the blessings you now enjoy. List your five major concerns and note what progress has been made. Have *you* been changed?

HORTICULTURE: A general rule is to plant twice as many seeds as you think you will need to allow for those that fail to germinate or to make it through the transplanting procedures. Seeds planted directly outdoors will not have as high a germination rate as seeds started indoors; expect about sixty percent yield.

Grass on the Roof

May all who hate Zion be turned back in shame.
May they be like grass on the roof, which withers
before it can grow; with it the reaper cannot fill
his hands, nor the one who gathers fill his arms.
May those who pass by not say, "The blessing of
the LORD be upon you; we bless you in the name
of the LORD"

—*PSALM 129:5–8*

We had two bare places in the lawn that defied seeding. So we laid five mats of sod that have done very well, but only because we first loosened the ground and then watered every day. It is amazing how quickly healthy, lush sod dries up if it isn't watered.

The grass on the roof mentioned in this passage does not refer to the kind of thatched roofs similar to English country houses. Thatch does not grow. This grass would be little tufts, having sprouted on the roof from seeds blown there by the wind and lodged in some protected corner. For a short time a few blades might spring up, but in the hot, dry climate of Palestine, the grass would quickly wither.

The psalmist prayed that the enemies of Zion, God's people, would be so ineffective and powerless that they would expire quickly, long before any harvest was possible. Those who hated Zion were so shameful, so ridiculous in their boastful pride, he declared, that they did not merit even the most casual blessing.

Today the church is still under attack, and it seems as if the enemies are more powerful and more deeply entrenched than ever. Surely, Christians who were imprisoned in formerly communist countries wondered if they would ever be freed. Fortunately, the faithful prayers of other Christians around the world have been answered.

We need not despair when anti-Christian forces seem to gain the upper hand. They are like grass on a roof, whose time of growth and vigor will be brief. God will have his victory in his time.

HEARTICULTURE: Pray for Christian leaders and organizations that are being attacked in the media. Write a letter of encouragement to one of them.

HORTICULTURE: Do not mow newly sodded lawn, as the mat can be pulled up from its base. More importantly, the top growth of two to three inches aids in the development of new root systems. The longer grass of a sodded area may temporarily look unattractive, but allowing it to grow undisturbed for a few weeks before mowing will result in healthier grass in the long run.

Just a Small Garden

*My heart is not proud, O LORD, my eyes are not
haughty; I do not concern myself with great matters or things too wonderful for me. But I have
stilled and quieted my soul; like a weaned child
with its mother, like a weaned child is my soul
within me. O Israel, put your hope in the LORD
both now and forevermore.*

—PSALM 131

It was my father, not my mother, who was the
family gardener, so I was surprised when
Mother, at age eighty, became interested in flowers. Each
year thereafter she did three things. She placed an urn full
of red geraniums on either side of her front door, filled a
half barrel with marigolds at the end of the driveway, and
planted impatiens at the back edge of her lot.

Mother never expanded into planting spring-flow-
ering bulbs nor did she ever sow zinnias. She had neither
skill, strength, nor interest in anything beyond her traditional spring efforts. But those few flowers gave her great
pleasure, and she was content.

The picture of a sloping backyard, banked with
perennials, all carefully positioned as to size, color, and
time of bloom, can arouse in the true gardener's heart the
desire to duplicate such beauty. A modest hobby unexpect-
edly becomes a full-time occupation. And taking on such a
project can produce great frustration if money or strength
runs out before completion.

Most people long to do something spectacular. In this passage, however, David describes a person who has learned how to be content with less than remarkable achievement. He defines true peace as a state similar to that of a weaned child who is no longer dependent upon his mother's milk. Although his tastes haven't changed and he still prefers milk, he can exist without it.

Contentment is knowing our place—like my mother with her geraniums.

HEARTICULTURE: Paul wrote the Philippians that he had learned to be content, whatever the circumstances (Phil. 4:11). What was his secret? The Lord, who gave him strength. Paul's hope was rightly placed.

HORTICULTURE: A realistic start for any landscaping plan is to list the available resources in money, time, skill, and the actual growing conditions in the yard. A five-year plan reduces the pressure to do everything at once, and offers the great advantage of having a cut-off point.

Ho Hum, Rain Again

*Sing to the LORD with thanksgiving; make music
to our God on the harp. He covers the sky with
clouds; he supplies the earth with rain and makes
grass grow on the hills. He provides food for the
cattle and for the young ravens when they call.*
—PSALM 147:7–9

A few years ago we had a drought here in the
Midwest that devastated the grain crops. In
August, the corn was only two feet high. Soybean plants
stood yellowed and sere. Cattle were already eating hay
intended for the winter. The Lord did not cover the sky
with clouds or supply the earth with rain, and any ravens
who called were disappointed!

Why did the Lord hold back the water that was so
essential? Perhaps it was because we had grown unappreciative. We had been taking rain for granted, as something
God was supposed to provide because we deserved it. We
had forgotten to say, "Thank you."

Or perhaps we needed to take a fresh look at the
Lord's goodness. Rain had lost its luster for us. We had
stopped marveling at how clean the world was after a
shower, how green the grass, how sweet the air. Ho hum,
same old weather forecast.

But the drought brought us together. It was a
"when all else fails, call the doctor" approach, but prayer
was finally acknowledged as the answer to our problem.

From all over the Midwest, Christians came together to seek forgiveness for past ingratitude and to plead for rain.

And the Lord answered! Showers revived a wide area. We were revived too, as we experienced the blessing of knowing that God did care about us.

HEARTICULTURE: It is a common practice today to ascribe weather to the meteorologists who forecast it. "Well, Dave, what kind of a weekend are you going to give us?" People make such comments in a lighthearted manner, perhaps, but the implication is clear that the person who predicts the weather has something to do with what it will be. Those who know the Lord as the Commander of weather forces have a natural and wonderful opportunity to witness to his power.

HORTICULTURE: Increasing interest is being given to planting flowers that are drought-tolerant. Some of the many annuals available are Rose Moss, Gazania, Dusty Miller, African Daisy, Mexican Sunflower, and Coreopsis. Perennials include Missouri Primrose, Potentilla, Geum, Sedum, Malva, Monarda, and Euphorbia.

If at First You Don't Succeed, Don't Try Again!

How useless to spread a net in full view of all the birds!

—*Proverbs 1:17*

A gardener once told me that he wouldn't mind the birds pecking his tomatoes so much if they wouldn't peck each tomato only once. It seems that birds never go back for second helpings!

The farmer in biblical times had the same problem. In this humorous proverb, we can picture the birds aligned along the fence, watching with delight as the farmer covers his grapes with a net. They will quickly perceive where there are gaps and are just waiting for the right moment to swoop down and eat their fill.

There exists a conflict between instinct and judgment. Birds will respond as birds, making up in persistence what they lack in creative thinking. On the other hand, human beings have been endowed with the ability to examine a situation and make necessary adjustments. To do this, we need to be open to various possibilities and then be willing to change our behavior.

The old motto, "If at first you don't succeed, try, try again," is not always good advice. Some situations call for an alternative solution. For example, some plants will not grow under certain conditions, no matter how gorgeous the pictures in a catalog. I always plant the potted chrysanthemums sold in the supermarket, but they never come through for me. When will I learn to enjoy them for a month on the front porch and then toss them back into the compost?

Relationships with loved ones, church programs, our personal health regime—all these and other matters need to be examined from time to time. As we age, circumstances change, and so must we.

HEARTICULTURE: How can Christians make sound judgments? God gives believers his Word, the Bible. He also gives us the Holy Spirit to guide and teach us. A third source of wisdom is a Christian friend. "If any of you lacks wisdom, he should ask God, who gives generously to all without finding fault, and it will be given to him" (James 1:5).

HORTICULTURE: Gardening supply companies now sell a knitted polyethylene netting which can be laid directly over plants or supported by wire hoops. The netting is also useful for protecting young seedlings from harsh sunlight. Bird netting, in sizes from 4 x 50 to 13 x 39, is large enough to be placed over bushes and trees.

God's Sense-of-Humor Vegetable

Honor the LORD with your wealth, with the first-fruits of all your crops; then your barns will be filled to overflowing, and your vats will brim over with new wine.

—PROVERBS 3:9–10

My neighbor is letting me use half her vegetable garden, so for the first time in many years, I have a sunny spot for growing zucchini. Knowing the possibility of squash vine borers, I put in three plants.

Zucchini is God's sense-of-humor vegetable. It either grows in abundance or not at all. If you plant one seedling, it will die. If you plant sixty seedlings, all will flourish.

It's easy to give away the first tender zucchini from your garden. In the early days of summer they make delightful gifts. But by late July, if you arrive at church with a bulky paper sack in your hand, people scatter like bugs when the light is turned on. And sick friends hope you won't find out they're ill, for fear you will bless them with another zucchini casserole or two more loaves of zucchini bread!

God wants the firstfruits of all our crops—not just the easy-to-grow zucchini, but also the exotic vegetables we don't tell anyone about. Out of our gratitude for all God has done for us and in trust that he will supply our needs, we are to offer him the first harvest, the best we have to give.

HEARTICULTURE: The Bible sets the minimum amount that we give to God as ten percent. Those who are struggling financially now may not see how they can be so generous. But God promises that when we give him a tithe of our income, he will bless us. "'Test me in this,' says the LORD Almighty, 'and see if I will not throw open the flood-gates of heaven and pour out so much blessing that you will not have room enough for it'" (Mal. 3:10).

HORTICULTURE: Tests by the United States Department of Agriculture have proven that the use of black plastic mulch benefits zucchini tremendously, especially when used in combination with drip irrigation. Prepare the soil first, spread out the black plastic, anchor it firmly to the soil, and cut holes for the seeds or trans-plants.

Offensive Landscaping

Do not plot harm against your neighbor, who lives trustfully near you.

—PROVERBS 3:29

The word used for *harm* in this proverb can be something as devastating as burning your neighbor's house down or throwing a rock through her picture window. More likely, however, *harm* translates into "a long-term annoyance," such as the neighbor's tree that drops its sticky fruit all over your driveway or the person who doesn't rake his leaves, but lets them blow into the yard next door.

Here in the Midwest, where houses are built on flood plains with little thought given to drainage, a common solution to leaky basements is to attach a fat black hose to the drain pipes so that water is carried away from the house. Sometimes the hose is buried, with only one end sticking up at the bottom of a hill. Often the hose is simply laid on top of the ground, with the water eventually draining onto a lower level. Either way, this runoff can "trespass" on a neighbor's property!

Certain plants cannot be contained and spill over onto adjoining land. Mint and lemon balm send their runners at will. Zoysia grass knows no boundaries. The roots of willow trees seek out moisture, a problem when the dampness surrounds water pipes. We had our willow tree cut down rather than cause any more water backup in our neighbor's washing machine.

Significant also is the verb *plot*, which indicates a *conscious* design to be hurtful, although we must not excuse what may be a basic lack of concern for other people. Meanwhile, the neighbor is living trustfully, assuming that all is going well between herself and the people next door.

Those of us who love the Lord have an obligation to plan our landscaping so that others are not harmed in any way. When our neighbor offends us, there is ample scriptural direction for settling the dispute in a fair and friendly manner.

HEARTICULTURE: Paul tells us that "each of us should please his neighbor for his good, to build him up" (Rom. 15:2). Going beyond the law that states we should not *harm* our neighbors, what can a gardener do to *please* them?

HORTICULTURE: Bishop's Weed (*aegopodium podagrari*) can be controlled by shearing off the blossoms before seeds form. Another means of controlling this indomitable plant is to cover it with a thick mulch.

Planning Our Steps

Make level paths for your feet and take only ways that are firm.

—PROVERBS 4:26

Our three bird feeders stand on a slight slope about fifteen feet from the house. Early in January our area suffered a most unusual freeze. Everything was covered with a thick sheet of ice. When the time came to fill the bird feeders, my husband managed to slide down to them. But getting back up the slope was another matter! There was no traction whatsoever.

Rather than leave him out there until we had a thaw, I took a plastic pail and tied it to a long rope. I attached the other end of the rope to our gas grill. Positioning myself firmly next to the grill, I tossed the pail to my husband while gripping the secured end. He then worked his way, hand over hand, back to the patio. The next day he chipped a line of steps from the patio to the feeder.

It is God's desire that our decisions be made in accordance with his will. The steps we take to achieve this goal begin with a vision of what we can accomplish with God's help. Turning this vision into action demands practical planning—analyzing possible pitfalls or dangers before proceeding.

This proverb implies that if there is no "firm" way, we should not take it. While our freeze continued, many people had to stay home. Even going out to the mailbox was too hazardous. There are occasions when we should simply stay put.

HEARTICULTURE: We read in Isaiah 30:21: "Whether you turn to the right or to the left, your ears will hear a voice behind you, saying, 'This is the way, walk in it.'" God is ready to guide us if we ask him.

HORTICULTURE: Steps and walkways should be made of materials that harmonize with those used elsewhere in the landscape. For example, the rustic look of railroad ties is incompatible with the formal appearance of a brick patio. Instead, try brick steps, or edge concrete steps with brick. Steps made of wood work well with a wood deck, or informally planted area. On the other hand, large stones, by their cut and texture, complement both a formal or informal setting.

The Best Apples of All

*Keep my commands and you will live; guard my
teachings as the apple of your eye.*
—*PROVERBS 7:2*

Since the rule for luggage on the airplane was
three pieces, I approached the check-in counter
at the airport in Albany with trepidation. I had two suitcases and two boxes, each containing a bushel of apples.
When the clerk eyed my excess with concern, I explained,
"These are New York state apples. They're the best in the
world. We can't buy them in St. Louis." New York apples?
Oh, well, that made all the difference. On the belt they
went. Not even an extra charge.

Shopping for apples is a ritual my brother and I
observe every year when I go home for a visit. From the
dozens of varieties piled up in the roadside market, we
choose four. We start with MacIntosh to eat right away, and
end up with Cortlands, which are good keepers. The
remaining two vary, depending upon the time of year and
growing conditions. Northern Spies, Winesaps, Baldwins—
all vie for attention.

The pupil of the eye is called an "apple," because it
is the center, the key. Of all the parts of our body, the pupil
is the most delicate. We are to guard jealously God's teachings with the same intensity we employ to protect our eyes.

"To guard" does not mean to seal our Bible in a
waterproof bag. The implication here is to keep God's
Word intact, free from worldly interpretation, to do exactly

what it says, and to prove we have taken divine advice by living a changed life.

With the proverb comes a promise: "You will live." Possibly longer. Certainly more happily. Definitely forever after death.

HEARTICULTURE: Consider each of the Ten Commandments in Exodus 20. How would keeping each one relate to a longer, happier life?

HORTICULTURE: Dwarf apple trees are advertised as the perfect choice for the home orchard. Take into account that dwarfs are somewhat less hardy and therefore not as well suited to colder climates. They also need more fertile soil and must be staked, as their roots do not provide enough anchorage. Semi-dwarfs do not have these problems.

Roses Need Attention

Lazy hands make a man poor, but diligent hands bring wealth.

—Proverbs 10:4

The film on how to grow roses was clear and comprehensive. In seven segments the expert rose grower explained everything the average person would need to know—from buying bare root versus potted plants to arranging fresh flowers.

The narrator insisted that roses are not difficult to grow. "Just follow a few basic rules of maintenance and prevention," he declared. "It only takes a few minutes a day."

He then demonstrated proper soil preparation ("a few minutes"), planting ("a few minutes"), watering ("a few minutes"), feeding ("a few minutes"), pruning ("a few minutes"), and treatment for insects and disease ("a few minutes"). "I don't think I want to grow roses," my husband commented when the film was over. "All those few minutes add up to a lot of time!"

Roses, it is true, need attention. You can't just plop them in the ground and let them make their own way. However, the result of all your diligence is considered by many to be the supreme flower. If you don't want to bother, grow marigolds. For little effort, you will produce a nice little flower. But it won't be a rose!

HEARTICULTURE: Wealth and poverty transcend financial concepts. Laziness practiced by a rich person makes him poor in the sense that he misses God's blessing. Work was one of the joys of paradise, as recorded in Genesis 2:15, for there is a reward in producing something useful and beautiful.

HORTICULTURE: All-America Rose Selections, Inc., recommends that rose growers in areas where temperatures dip below five degrees in the winter, cut back rose plants to about twenty-four inches after the first hard frost. Tie the canes together and form a six- to eight-inch mound of fresh, loose soil or compost around the base. Leave until spring when new growth is observed. Then carefully remove the soil mounds and prune back.

Dream Garden?

He who works his land will have abundant food,
but he who chases fantasies lacks judgment.
                                                    —PROVERBS 12:11

I had great plans for the newly tilled plot at the bottom of the hill. Asparagus, of course, peas, beans, five different root crops, lettuce, cabbage, broccoli, squash, tomatoes (four varieties), and peppers, both sweet and hot.

My husband borrowed a Rototiller to cut through the giant clods of clay that had lain undisturbed for twenty years. All I had to do was take out a thousand rocks, add compost, rake it smooth, and plant. On the second day of this labor, I eliminated the asparagus. On the third day, I gave up the peas. I realized I would never see a green bean if I didn't erect a fence to keep out the rabbits. When the next hard rain washed right through the area set aside for zucchini, I had to lay railroad ties.

My "dream" garden was well-named. I just couldn't support it with the work required. Reality produced two crops of green beans and a few tomatoes.

Between television and sophisticated graphics, we are surrounded by fantasy. We want to be thin without eating less. We want to win a war without casualties. We buy lottery tickets and dream of spending fourteen million dollars.

Over and over again, God's Word reminds us that our needs will be supplied through hard work. To recognize this is evidence of good judgment.

HEARTICULTURE: How does faith differ from fantasy? It takes judgment to distinguish between the two! Romans 10:17 says, "Consequently, faith comes from hearing the message, and the message is heard through the word of Christ." Faith is always linked to the Scriptures. Fantasy is not.

HORTICULTURE: The rigid rules of vegetable gardening, requiring carefully laid-out rows for seeds and plants, have been relaxed in favor of mixing vegetables with flowers that respond to similar conditions. This allows a small family to plant a variety of vegetables without being overwhelmed. A bed of sun-loving flowers may include two tomato plants. A few red lettuce plants add a contrasting note to sunny marigolds. Green peppers can provide a background for petunias—even in the front yard!

The Diligent Gardener

The sluggard craves and gets nothing, but the
desires of the diligent are fully satisfied.
—PROVERBS 13:4

A recent newspaper story featuring an out-
standing local garden stated that the owner was
up at dawn and often worked throughout the day. You
could drive by the yard almost any time, and there would
be the diligent gardener—back bent—fertilizing, snipping,
weeding. No wonder she had a prizewinner!

Few of us can spend every day, all day, working in
our yards. There is a difference, we say, between being diligent and being obsessed. Our level of determination
depends upon our desires. We may not want to be written
up in the newspaper, or win a prize. An attractive landscape with enough blooms for household bouquets may be
good enough for some of us. Nor do we necessarily have
to grow the largest tomato or the longest green bean. A
consistent supply of vegetables to feed the family is just
fine, thank you.

The diligent person works toward a goal. The sluggard, on the other hand, craves results, but does not want
to make the effort to achieve them. She really should mow
the lawn and prune the hedges. The oak tree branches
that block the sidewalk should be cut off. Maybe tomorrow,
when it's not so hot.

To appreciate fully the impact of this verse in
Proverbs, we should alter it to read: "The desires of the

soul of the diligent," for God is really speaking about spiritual matters. He wants us to be diligent in seeking food for our soul and in actively serving the Lord. A lazy approach to personal devotions, neglect of public worship, or apathy toward ministry will not bring us to that sweet fellowship with God that our souls ultimately need to be satisfied.

HEARTICULTURE: Diligence is constant and earnest effort. This definition contradicts the notion that we can experience spiritual growth through an occasional skimming of Bible verses or a quick prayer. How faithful are you in the tending of your own devotional garden? What kind of relationship with God do you desire?

HORTICULTURE: "Weekend gardeners" who produce great gardens admit that they plan extensively and make heavy use of such work-saving measures as mulch, paved walkways, containers, and . . . realistic ambitions! For those who have the time, a half-hour of daily attention to a garden is worth an entire Saturday.

Seeing Is Not Always Believing!

A simple man believes anything, but a prudent man gives thought to his steps.
—*PROVERBS 14:15*

In seed catalogs there are no failures. Every plant is luscious, bursting with good health. One company advertises petunias that are seven inches wide. Another shows a man holding up a green bean that reaches to the ground. One is assured that anyone can grow a six-hundred-pound pumpkin, but the information on how to move this behemoth is missing.

The steps for producing a healthy plant begin by counting back to when the seed should first be set in the soil. For the person who uses florescent lights indoors, this involves four to six weeks of care before the plants can be set outside. If you sow directly in the ground, consider the last date for frost in your area, temperature, moisture, wind, soil composition, and all the information on the back of the seed packet.

Even after all these steps have been taken, a lot of faith must accompany the planting of a seed. This is a faith based upon past experience and reasonable assurance, however.

The simple (minded) person thinks everything he hears or sees is true. When his foolishness is confined to the purchase of a few seed packets, relatively little harm is done. But when he falls for every idle voice that would affect his soul, he puts himself in great danger. It is the prudent—the wise and careful—person who compares every religious teaching with the truth of God's Word. The steps she then takes are based upon this completely reliable guide.

HEARTICULTURE: In Ephesians 4:13, we read that we are to grow up, "attaining to the whole measure of the fullness of Christ." God has given us his Word, as well as pastors and teachers who believe it, to help us mature in our faith.

HORTICULTURE: When examining a seed catalog, consider first of all the location of the company. One major supplier from the East Coast is really in England, which means its promises are based upon the coolness and moisture of the English climate. Seeds originating in Maine or Oregon may not respond the same way in Georgia. On the other hand, live plants grown in your own region are already acclimated to your growing conditions.

Looking for That Miracle Seed

All hard work brings a profit, but mere talk leads only to poverty.
—*Proverbs 14:23*

The picture on the can showed a field of wild-flowers—Missouri Primrose, Blue Flax, Blanket Flower, Phlox—sixteen varieties in all. The gardener is instructed to plant these on a suburban hillside for the new "natural" look. Since the flowers are "wild," one assumes that planting is a simple matter of taking a hand-ful of seeds from the can and scattering them casually about on the wind. This image of the sower is totally com-patible with the image of the colorful meadow. Add two lit-tle girls with their arms full of posies, and the picture is irresistible.

A closer reading of the directions on the can reveals that you must precede your strewing with some hard work. The ground must be prepared. Stones need to be raked up and the soil tilled. Once the seeds are in the ground, they must be covered ever so lightly and tamped down. Light watering is essential. Even when everything is done correctly, the fine print admits you won't get a good crop until the second year.

What the seed companies *don't* tell you is that a heavy rain before the seeds sprout may cause them all to wash down to the bottom of the hill, where they pop up en masse in your perennial bed. Or they may get too wet or too dry and don't pop up at all! If the seeds *do* sprout, you may not be able to count sixteen different kinds.

Every gardener would like at least one miracle seed that produces a bed of mature flowers six weeks later. Weed- and insect-free, of course! Cultivation is hard work, particularly when the plot is full of stones or heavy with wet clay.

Anything worthwhile takes cultivating, however. Marriage, children, friendships, business and professional contacts, church membership, neighborhood relationships—all require faithful attention. Weeds of discord must be pulled out, the fertilizer of love applied, the water of forgiveness sprinkled as needed. And then the gardener must exercise patience, knowing that the plants need to mature before they can bear fruit. There is always the waiting along with the work.

HEARTICULTURE: A senior high youth leader was asked how she put up with a certain group of teenagers, since they seemed so difficult to manage. "I think of what they will become, and not what they are now" was her wise reply.

HORTICULTURE: Deep tilling is not suited to the sowing of wildflower seeds. Unwanted weeds are encouraged to grow rapidly, crowding out the flowers. Rake the area no more than one-half inch deep. Combine the seed with a carrier such as sand, topsoil, or potting soil and broadcast carefully.

Even Impatiens Take Patience!

A patient man has great understanding, but a
quick-tempered man displays folly.
—*Proverbs 14:29*

Slice a tulip bulb in half, and you will find the entire plant encapsulated. Look carefully, and you can see the flower, leaves, and stem. A seed is even more amazing, for in it resides an entire plant in the form of a combination of genes and chromosomes, invisible to the naked eye.

There is no way we can pull the tulip out of the bulb or bring a full-grown plant immediately out of the seed. Germination and growth to fruition take a certain amount of time, even under optimum conditions. Nothing teaches patience like gardening!

Note that patience follows understanding. Once we know how a person or a thing operates, we can allow it to follow its course. The first year I planted caladiums, I was ready to dig up the entire bed when nothing appeared for four weeks. It was early summer before the tightly wrapped leaves broke through the ground.

Children follow a certain course of growth. Parents and teachers who learn the capabilities of different age groups do not set up unrealistic expectations. Understanding the background of a person—why she acts like she does—enables us to accept her behavior. Of course, patience *without* understanding is stronger evidence of control by the Holy Spirit.

The quick-tempered person, in contrast, allows passion to take the place of reason. Things must work properly the first time. Things must work *now*. The quick-tempered person cannot differentiate between things and people and may treat a balky child in the same abusive manner he uses with a balky lawnmower.

Note that the quick-tempered person *displays* her folly. She cannot conceal the anger that is the basis of her impatience. The sin that God sees is thus revealed to everyone else, for rarely can impatience be disguised. We may not speak angrily or act impulsively, but tightly set lips and a rigidly controlled tone of voice are dead give-aways.

HEARTICULTURE: Would you describe yourself as an impatient person? Read Galatians 5:16–26 to see how God views this aspect of our sinful nature. Help to overcome it is given in the third chapter of Colossians.

HORTICULTURE: The most common mistake made by gardeners is planting already blooming annuals before the climate and soil have warmed sufficiently. Remember that soil temperature is usually ten degrees lower than air temperature.

Seasoned With Love

Better a little with the fear of the LORD than
great wealth with turmoil. Better a meal of veg-
etables where there is love than a fattened calf
with hatred.

—PROVERBS 15:16–17

To the person who thinks the greatest feast in the world is the first harvest of sweet corn or a tomato picked and eaten right in the garden, a fattened calf doesn't hold much appeal anyway. A growing number of people, no pun intended, are vegetarians by choice.

When this proverb was written, meat was not a regular part of the diet. The fattened calf was served only on special occasions and, to this day, symbolizes the extra effort merited by an honored guest. But we've all attended at least one dinner where the food was great, and the company terrible. The tastiness of the steaks grilled on the patio went unnoticed in the midst of sarcastic, cutting remarks.

By contrast, love makes the poorest food delicious. Parents who seek solid happiness for their children will teach them to put little emphasis upon acquiring worldly things and great emphasis upon developing Christ-like attributes. It is the atmosphere in a household that matters, not the furniture . . . or the menu.

Paul reminded Timothy that "godliness with contentment is great gain. For we brought nothing into the world, and we can take nothing out of it" (1 Tim. 6:6).

Contentment with simple things in a world obsessed with materialism is a condition that is achieved only by giving diligent attention to scriptural teachings and prayer. Nor is it a permanent condition once it is realized. Continuing cultivation is necessary. Not unlike a vegetable garden.

HEARTICULTURE: For many families, the evening meal is the only time of the day when everyone is together, and even that event can be preempted by dozens of other activities. Certain nights of the week may have to be set aside as inviolate. What can be done to make these family times happy ones?

HORTICULTURE: The simplest and best way to control weeds is to hoe them every week or so, or whenever a new batch appears. Don't cultivate too deeply, or you run the risk of harming the roots of your vegetable plants and bringing new weed seeds to the surface, where they can sprout.

A Leaky Hose

*Commit to the LORD whatever you do, and your
plans will succeed.*
                                        —PROVERBS 16:3

For Mother's Day my husband gave me hose.
This particular kind is light green and fifty feet
long. Before that, I had a black rubber hose over twenty
years old. When it developed a slit about halfway back
from the nozzle, I was able to water two places in the front
yard at the same time. Then two more holes appeared.
After careful arranging, I could water four areas at once,
which resulted in an artistic fountain display between the
trees, but very little water coming out of the nozzle.

My carefully placed system fell apart the evening I
gave the lawn its semiannual feed and weed. As I walked
back and forth, spraying the grass, water began to pelt me
from all sides. One look at my drenched pants, and my
husband decided the old black hose had to go.

Do we not, sometimes, feel burdened to accomplish some worthy task for the Lord's glory and proceed
with great energy toward that end? However, as time goes
by, our drive is dissipated by various lesser objectives. We
take on a job here, a responsibility there, forcing us either
to delay the completion of our goal or to lower our standards.

Diversion is the Devil's tactic. If he can keep us
from succeeding in our objective, even with worthy but less
important demands, he has succeeded. He knows that a

leaky hose, which may have its advantages, is never as effective as a strong hose that does one thing well.

HEARTICULTURE: Before we say yes to any suggested responsibility, we need to pray for guidance. This delay also gives us time to seek counsel from a trusted friend, as well as to examine our own priorities and limitations. Most of our overcommitment is due to pressure to make an immediate decision.

HORTICULTURE: A lawn can be maintained without much extra water. Although unattractive to some, a lawn that is brown and dormant in summer is not dead. It will usually bounce back to greenness in the fall. To keep grass green, however, water only once every seven to ten days during dry periods, but water deeply. An inch of water a week is adequate for Midwestern soils. Use a rain gauge or straight-sided can marked to that depth.

Storm in the Stationery Store

When a king's face brightens, it means life; his favor is like a rain cloud in spring.
—PROVERBS 16:15

Considering the small number of absolute monarchs in the world today, this proverb seems to lack much application. But when we expand the definition of "king" to include anyone who has the power to bring misery or happiness to certain people, most of us would have to admit that we ourselves have played the role of petty tyrants at one time or another.

By this definition, parents are kings. So are teachers, bosses, military commanders, coaches, club leaders, and so on, since people in these roles often determine the climate for those under their authority. A cheerful king brings zest and vitality to everyone under his command. A gloomy, critical, or negative attitude in a leader creates an atmosphere in which enthusiasm dies.

I once shopped in a stationery store where the manager was openly critical of his clerks. When the woman helping me had difficulty finding a certain product in a catalog, he rudely took over. I left, feeling angry and embarrassed for the clerk. I stopped going to that store, and evidently many others did also. It is now closed.

A rain cloud in spring assures a more abundant crop. A leader's happy disposition encourages higher productivity from those under his authority.

HEARTICULTURE: Whatever may be the disposition of our earthly leaders, those under the rule of the King of Kings will experience his loving smile every day and eventually the incomparable brightness of heaven.

HORTICULTURE: While rainfall is never totally predictable, regional precipitation tables are useful in determining the best times for planting large crops.

Eating Our Words

From the fruit of his mouth a man's stomach is filled; with the harvest from his lips he is satisfied.

—*Proverbs 18:20*

When I became serious about growing green beans, I was amazed at the possibilities—size, color, shape, with or without strings, bush, climbers. Then I came across a company that sold nothing but bean seeds. There were beans for every regional taste, for drying, even for mosaics!

Since we "sow" many more words than we do seeds, it is infinitely more important what quality they are. We are well acquainted with the affect our words have on other people. Note that in this proverb the point made is that our words affect *us*. To repeat an old adage, "We may have to eat our words."

To be "satisfied"—in fellowship with God and consequently with other people—I will heed the scriptural injunctions to speak loving, comforting, encouraging, helpful words. I will not gossip or say anything unkind, harmful, or of unsound counsel. God promises to bless my wholesome speech with the same feeling of well-being one experiences at the end of a fine dinner.

HEARTICULTURE: We read in James 3:6 that the tongue "corrupts the whole person." Could our heartburn or headache relate in any way to words that have been spoken out of anger or bitterness? Would a restored relationship with someone we have offended improve our digestion?

HORTICULTURE: For a succession of plantings of bush snap beans, let the size of the last-planted bean row be your guide. Sow your next row when the second level of leaves forms on the plants. In most climates you can plant seven or eight rows.

Valuable Junk

The purposes of a man's heart are deep waters,
but a man of understanding draws them out.
—PROVERBS 20:5

The first Tuesday after the new hose was hooked up, my husband stuffed the old one in a garbage can and set it out on the curb, ready for our semi-weekly trash removal. I was working in the side yard after lunch and noted that the can was empty. Thinking the truck had come, I went around front to put our cans in the garage. To my surprise I discovered that, while the other garbage was still there, someone had driven by and taken the hose!

Our curiosity was aroused. What does one do with a leaky rubber hose? Cut out the good portion and couple it to another hose? Make a rubber bumper for a boat dock? Insert wire in it and use it as a brace for a new tree? I've often wished the person or persons who needed that hose had just stopped by and asked for it, so we wouldn't have to wonder what they were going to do with that old piece of junk.

Years ago, there was a popular saying intended to build one's self-esteem: "God don't make no junk." No one is worthless in God's creation. Each of us is important to him and has a purpose.

We can't always learn what makes a person "tick." Often we have to be understanding without the opportunity to draw him or her out. For example, we may not ever know that the waitress who just spilled coffee on our skirt is awaiting a divorce decree. Or that the mediocre performance by the clerk in the supermarket represents progress, compared with what he was able to do before he underwent drug therapy.

It helps us to be gracious if we remember that there is no human trash.

HEARTICULTURE: What group of people showed less promise than Jesus' disciples? They were obtuse, lacking in faith, and jealous of each other. Peter was the worst of all! But out of this group of twelve came eleven men who formed the human backbone of a religion that has changed the world.

HORTICULTURE: Garlic has as many uses in the garden as it does in the kitchen. Planted near roses, it can aid in fighting black spot. A spray of garlic cloves and water, mixed in a blender, combats various insects and blights. Add a tablespoon of oil to the mixture to help it cling.

Flooding God's Field

A king's heart is in the hand of the LORD; he
directs it like a watercourse wherever he pleases.
—PROVERBS 21:1

My son's father-in-law, who is an accomplished handyman, has gone into water gardening in a big way. He can, with a flick of a switch, produce a waterfall cascading down the hill next to his house. This forms a stream, ending in a pool covered by a footbridge. Shiny orange carp swim underneath the bridge, while a nearby fountain spouts three feet high.

Water garden technology can now produce an instant watercourse of any kind and size, able to go where the gardener pleases. In Solomon's time, when this proverb was written, however, a watercourse began as a tiny spring, to be joined by other streams. When the stream reached bottomland, the farmer was able to direct its course to irrigate his crops.

A king of this era was considered to be the ultimate authority, almost a god. But God says he directs earthly kings to serve *his* purposes. As George F. Santa wrote, "Kings, in pursuing their chosen courses, flooded or fertilized God's field as He chose."

Joseph, Nehemiah, and Daniel exerted their influence as God directed their rulers. Tiglath-pileser, Cyrus, and Artaxerxes, therefore, were acting as God had ordained. Government heads today are no less part of God's master plan to bring his kingdom into full fruition.

HEARTICULTURE: In 1 Timothy 2:1–2 we are urged to pray for those in authority. The purpose of these prayers is to ensure believers the right to "live peaceful and quiet lives in all godliness and holiness"—in other words, to practice their faith.

HORTICULTURE: Waterfalls and fountains soothe the spirit, since moving water is therapeutic and cooling. The turbulence of pumps helps to add oxygen and release carbon dioxide from the water, a help to ornamental fish. Water lilies, however, need still water, and should be planted in quiet pools, away from waterfalls and fountains.

Boundaries Are a Blessing!

*Do not move an ancient boundary stone set up by
your forefathers.*

—*Proverbs 22:28*

For many of us, the most ancient boundary
stone we ever have to deal with is the line
between our property and that of the house next door.
And we don't pay much attention to that until we decide to
erect a fence or lay out a garden. Dogs and zoysia grass
don't pay any attention to boundary lines at all!

Boundaries, in the form of principles established
by God, may not be taken so casually. These principles—
the Ten Commandments, Jesus' parables, and Paul's directions for the church—are the foundation of our spiritual
lives. Intended for our good, they are God's means of protecting us from our inherent evil intentions.

We need boundaries. We need to know how far we
can go. The results of lawlessness are reported by the news
media every day. Civil law, originating in scriptural law,
limits the behavior of every individual and makes him or
her responsible for the consequences.

The reference to our forefathers reminds us that
the law is not the property of any one generation. The
boundaries established for our ancestors still apply to us
today. We inherit these principles, just as we inherit the
exact dimensions of a piece of property, even though it
may date back hundreds of years.

HEARTICULTURE: The "do-your-own-thing" philosophy so heavily promoted today can affect Christians. We do not like to submit to authority, either! Psalm 16 tells us that God's boundaries are pleasant. Read it when you're feeling rebellious.

HORTICULTURE: Do you know where your property lines lie? We once owned an access road that was discovered to be two feet over on a neighbor's side! This discrepancy was of no concern to that neighbor at the time, but a change of ownership could present a serious problem. A survey is well worth the cost before undertaking major property changes. This is one way in which we show our love for our neighbor.

A Time to Plant

There is a time for everything, and a season for every activity under heaven: . . . a time to plant and a time to uproot.

—*ECCLESIASTES 3:1–2*

Geraniums appear in Midwestern markets in mid-April. In east central New York, where my brother gardens, Memorial Day is the traditional time for setting out geraniums. Here we can put in a second planting of vegetables as late as August, while he keeps an eye out for a Labor Day frost.

The proper time to plant is related not only to zone or time of year but depends upon the gardener's experience, situation, and inclination. Certain vegetables are not for the novice, as I learned when I set out celery.

We plant other things, too. There is the right time to plant an idea. Churches are planted, and this takes much prayer and organization. We hope to plant a love for the Lord in our children. We may also plant in them a love for learning, or music, or horses. We might plant a seed of kindness with the hope that it will bloom in an unkind heart.

Uprooting also has its proper time. The garden has to be cleaned up for winter. Decisions have to be made about plants that make no progress. I have a clematis that is the same size today as when I put it in the ground three years ago. Since I bought it while on a trip with a friend, it has such emotional significance I can't give it up, but it does not warrant the huge trellis to which it is tied.

Much harder to uproot are people. Moving to a new home or starting a new job is a traumatic experience. We may find it difficult to budge from our position on a dearly held issue, or our place as an officer of the board. Perhaps the hardest move of all is the one that takes us into a retirement center or a room with our daughter and her family. Indeed, stress comes when we move up, down, off, on, or in!

Encouragement comes with the knowledge that God "has made everything beautiful in its time." That God is in charge of our planting and uprooting gives both a divine purpose that transcends any pain or inconvenience.

HEARTICULTURE: "My times are in your hands," said David in Psalm 31:15. There is no better place for them to be!

HORTICULTURE: When determining the dates for planting seeds or transplants in your garden, consult a map showing the dates for the last spring frost and first fall frost in your area. Then use a chart, indicating the range of safe planting dates for each variety you plan to plant. Finally, take into account your particular situation. For example, a northern slope will take longer to warm up than one facing south.

"Runaway" Beans

The end of a matter is better than its beginning,
and patience is better than pride. Do not be
quickly provoked in your spirit, for anger resides
in the lap of fools.

—*ECCLESIASTES 7:8–9*

The garden plot my neighbor has given me for growing vegetables (with the promise that I will grow some okra just for him!) has a wire fence across the back. I planted runner beans there. Some of the seeds, although fresh, did not sprout, and those that did seemed unusually puny. I took the trouble to attach each vine to a string, anchored by a wooden clothespin and stretching up to the wire fence.

Other gardeners in our area had harvested two crops of green beans before my vines even produced flowers. I concentrated on other vegetables, assuming I would never see a runner bean. In early July, to my great surprise, those bean plants took off like the rockets at our city park fireworks display. By the middle of the month, I found handfuls of tasty beans. The vines became irrepressible, climbing over the fence and proceeding on like the infamous kudzu. And to think I had been tempted to pull up those weak-looking beans!

This passage in Ecclesiastes accurately portrays human response, for when we are frustrated, we get angry. Then we may act irrationally or lash out with hateful words. Losing our self-control, we refuse to follow a matter through to a wise, well-thought-out conclusion.

It is God's desire for us that we develop a long-term view of life's challenges, whether they be recalcitrant seeds or recalcitrant people. Patience, in the knowledge that God is working all things out for our good and his glory, will reveal in the end, that what happened was indeed better than the beginning.

HEARTICULTURE: What, or who, really provokes you? Admit it by writing the name down on paper. Read Galatians 5:22–26. Pray specifically for patience as a fruit of the Holy Spirit.

HORTICULTURE: Bush beans mature sooner than pole beans (ten to twenty days before harvest) and usually yield three or four pickings, whereas pole varieties yield numerous pickings over a longer time span. In both cases, regular and thorough picking is important because it causes the plants to continue to set pods longer.

Rainmaker

If clouds are full of water, they pour rain upon the earth. Whether a tree falls to the south or to the north, in the place where it falls, there will it lie. Whoever watches the wind will not plant; whoever looks at the clouds will not reap. As you do not know the path of the wind, or how the body is formed in a mother's womb, so you cannot understand the work of God, the Maker of all things.

—*ECCLESIASTES 11:3–5*

Historically, there have been some attempts to make rain, but no one has yet come up with a way to stop it once it has started. Nor can we prevent trees from falling. On a recent trip to the Grand Tetons, I commented on the large number of lodge pole pines, lying this way and that on the hillsides. There is something sad about a fallen tree. It would have looked tidier, and more scenic, if all those trees had been gathered up in a neat pile, but it would not have been ecologically prudent. Those decaying trees are part of the "back to earth" cycle essential to a healthy forest.

Some things we can do nothing about. Others require us to make a decision and act on it. We must be just as realistic in our appraisal of what we must accept as of what we can change. To beat our breasts after a sudden downpour washes out our marigold seeds (for the second time!) is as futile as lamenting a destructive patch of weeds we are too lazy to pull up.

A second reaction to life's uncertainties is not to do anything at all. Because of the vagaries of the weather, we just won't put in a crop. Who knows what the wind might bring? The ideal conditions we insist upon never arrive, and so we fail to achieve greatness because we fail to take a risk.

Verse five reminds us that much of life is unknown and unknowable. The marvel of the human body is beyond our comprehension, but babies continue to be conceived and born. We can but trust in God, the Maker of all things. He would have us step forth in faith.

HEARTICULTURE: The same Hebrew word for *wind* serves also for *spirit*. Being born again by the power of the Holy Spirit is an even greater mystery. Read John 3:1–21 and reflect on God's promises.

HORTICULTURE: One advantage of growing plants from seed is the low cost. So many tomatoes can be grown from one packet that a few can be set out early in the hope of favorable temperatures. If these plants do not survive, there are plenty more to be set out at the proper time.

Get On With the Job!

Sow your seed in the morning, and at evening let
not your hands be idle, for you do not know
which will succeed, whether this or that, or
whether both will do equally well.
                                    —ECCLESIASTES 11:6

Whether or not seeds do better when planted at high noon or at night under a full moon, get on with the job! Our true response to uncertainty should be to redouble our effort. There is much we do not understand. Our control of events is minimal, and hard times are very likely. But we are to bestir ourselves and get busy.

In Ephesians 6:13, Paul acknowledges that the days are evil, but directs us to make the most of every opportunity. In 2 Timothy 4:2, he tells us to be prepared, whatever the season. In 2 Corinthians 8:2, he uses the Macedonian church as an example of those believers who suffered severe trial and yet experienced overflowing joy.

The Scriptures do not call us to act irresponsibly or out of pride in our own capabilities. We do our work in total dependence on God, but we do our work. My husband serves on the board of a retirement center that recently dedicated a garden adjacent to its medical center. If the termination of life ever had immediate, practical meaning, it is here, but each spring new flowers are planted and old ones are refurbished. All the work is done by the residents of the medical center!

HEARTICULTURE: Is there something you've put off doing out of fear for the future? Make a list of others who will benefit from your action, even if you don't, and proceed. Read John 12:25.

HORTICULTURE: If it is not convenient to set out new plants when first purchased, plant them in a shaded area and keep them watered until you can find a permanent place for them. The plants will keep well in this condition. "Heeling in" is a process in which trees or plants are laid close together in a trench, at an angle. The roots are then covered and properly watered. Some plants can be carried over the winter in this manner.

The Jesus Flower

I am a rose of Sharon, a lily of the valleys. Like a lily among thorns is my darling among the maidens.

—SONG OF SONGS *2:1–2*

The popular chorus, "Everybody Ought to Know," says that Jesus is "the lily of the valley, he's the bright and morning star." The writer of those words, obviously interpreting Song of Songs as a picture of the great love between Christ and his church, describes the Lord as having the singular beauty of a lily.

To the American mind, "lily of the valley" immediately conjures up the image of an early spring plant with broad leaves and a stem of tiny white bells. But the biblical flower was probably a wild lily, such as the tiger lily, which grows in profusion to brighten a landscape otherwise noted for its briars and thistles. What a delightful picture of Jesus this is!

The "rose of Sharon" is thought to be a crocus, which would do well in the fertile coastal plain between Joppa and Caesarea as it existed in Solomon's time. Since there are wild roses in Israel today, you may use that picture, since no one really knows the exact flowers being described. What is important is the writer's description of his Lord as a person of great beauty.

If you had to describe Jesus as a flower, which one would you choose? He might be more like the spectacular gladiola or the regal iris. Some would probably liken him to a hybrid tea rose—a single stem bearing an absolutely perfect bloom. Someone else might choose a daffodil, bringing a note of cheer as the bleak winter merges into spring.

Ultimately, Jesus is indescribable. But we gardeners who love flowers have the advantage of intimate acquaintance with loveliness and perfection so that we can say, "This specimen is absolutely beautiful, but Jesus is <u>more</u> beautiful."

HEARTICULTURE: In Isaiah 53:2 we read that Jesus "had no beauty or majesty to attract us to him, nothing in his appearance that we should desire him." Jesus did not look like a handsome movie star. He was ordinary enough to escape notice in a crowd. It is *who* Jesus is, not how he looked, that gives him his rare beauty.

HORTICULTURE: Lily of the valley, or *Convallaria*, does not do well in the warmer climates denoted by zones eight through ten. However, pips (underground shoots sent up by its rhizomes) can be purchased through catalogs and forced at any time of year.

The Amazing Pepo

The Daughter of Zion is left like a shelter in a vineyard, like a hut in a field of melons, like a city under siege.

—ISAIAH 1:8

The first time I planted squash, I read that the seeds were to be placed in hills. I wondered why squash seeds had to be higher up than other vegetables, but I followed the instructions and carefully constructed six little mounds along one edge of my garden. Then I dropped three seeds into each mound. It was years later before I learned that a "hill" is really a group. After that, I felt terribly wise—a gardener who had truly arrived.

When the Bible speaks of melons, it means melons as we know them. But when it speaks of cucumbers, it may mean cucumbers or watermelons or gourds. We know that melons have been cultivated in Egypt for centuries, and at the time this passage was written, seven hundred years before the birth of Christ, fields were extensive enough to require a watchtower with a guard as protection against predators—man or beast.

These towers were temporary lean-tos or shacks, used only when the fruit was ripening. Isaiah uses the illustration to warn Israel, and especially Judah, that the watchtower will soon be nothing more than an isolated hut in a field, one step short of the complete devastation that occurred in Sodom and Gomorrah.

The Daughter of Zion, God's people, had forsaken the Lord; they had turned their backs on him. There had been no attempt to seek forgiveness or to clean out the corruption. So God was turning them over to the fierce Assyrians, who would devastate their land.

A ripening muskmelon can remind us that God is patient but will not endure our sinfulness forever. Either there is repentance, or there will be reckoning. Which do we choose?

HEARTICULTURE: If we persist in our sinful behavior, God may decide to let us endure its natural outcome, though he never deliberately hurts his people to "teach them a lesson." He is always ready to forgive us when we repent and to redirect us on a new path to restoration.

HORTICULTURE: Amaze your friends! Tell them that melons, cucumbers, and the like belong to the cucurbit family. The botanical name for the fruit of a cucurbit is a *pepo*. Amaze your friends even more by adding well-composted animal manure, bone meal, or other mineral fertilizers to your soil to produce strong, productive vines.

The Fruitful Vineyard

In that day—"Sing about a fruitful vineyard: I, the LORD, watch over it; I water it continually. I guard it day and night so that no one may harm it."

—*ISAIAH 27:2–3*

A friend of mine, whose backyard is terraced with grapevines, decries the fact that the foil-wrapped vines sold in local stores are the least suitable varieties to grow in this region. Many people buy grapes based on the picture on the bundle and are attracted to those that resemble the bunches in the supermarket. Thus it is that Thompson seedless grapes, which look so luscious on the package, seldom reproduce the same way in the home garden.

Any advice on grape culture begins with the admonition to "find out which variety of grape is best for your area." Begin by calling your local nurseryman who can order it for you. Remember, you must also erect an arbor on which your grapes will grow. Books on grape cultivation make such a point of this that it is obvious many people never think of it until they read the directions.

Grapes need care. Don't believe the garden writer who says all you have to do is prune them every year. As my *Cooperative Extension Bulletin* puts it: "Grapes respond to cultivation." They can be damaged by the grape berry moth and black rot. As for pruning, there is more to it than hacking off a few limbs after Christmas.

Isaiah knew his grapes. He acknowledged that a fruitful vineyard requires continual attention. He prophesied that at the end of the age, Israel, God's people, will flourish under the divine protection of their holy God.

There are times when the future of the church universal, or our own congregation in particular, looks bleak. We see nothing but failure. Here is God's promise that a day is coming when we shall bear huge bunches of sweet fruit.

HEARTICULTURE: God truly loves his church. In Malachi 3:17–18, he offers these words of reassurance: "They will be mine . . . in the day when I make up my treasured possession. I will spare them, just as in compassion a man spares his son who serves him. And you will again see the distinction between the righteous and the wicked, between those who serve God and those who do not." In church matters, we are cultivators, not harvesters. God calls us to work and to trust him with the results.

HORTICULTURE: For home fruit production, six to twelve grape plants are enough. Each mature plant should produce around fifteen pounds of fruit.

Agriculture 101

When a farmer plows for planting, does he plow continually? Does he keep on breaking up and harrowing the soil?

—ISAIAH 28:24

Tucked away in Isaiah is this amazing little passage about farming. How did the farmer in 700 B.C. know what to do? He couldn't take agriculture courses at Jerusalem University or contact his friendly cooperative extension agent in Gilead. The Scriptures tell us that he was instructed by God himself.

God taught the farmer by endowing him with wisdom—the desire to learn from the experience of others and then to apply his own common sense. Once the soil was prepared, it was time to stop plowing and start planting. All of this may be perfectly obvious to our farmers today. But way back in the beginning, skills had to be learned for the first time. It was God who led the farmer to bring forth his food from the ground "by the sweat of his brow."

Knowledge about farming that has been accumulated through the ages is vast, yet there is still the need to use common sense in individual situations. We must balance what the experts say against our own unique set of circumstances, then apply sound judgment.

We may dislike taking responsibility for our actions and wish we could place this burden on someone else (at least when we make the wrong decision!). But no scenario is quite like any other, and God's gift of common sense is often the determining factor between success and failure.

HEARTICULTURE: Do you have to make a major decision this week? Ask God to lead you to the best authority on the subject and then equip you with the good sense to use the information wisely.

HORTICULTURE: Before digging up the plot for the family garden, test the soil. If it is dry, water it well and wait two days. It should crumble easily in your hand before you till.

Caraway, Cummin,
and Cartwheels

*Caraway is not threshed with a sledge, nor is a
cartwheel rolled over cummin; caraway is beaten
out with a rod, and cummin with a stick. All this
also comes from the LORD Almighty, wonderful
in counsel and magnificent in wisdom.*
—ISAIAH 28:27, 29

Since both caraway and cummin are valuable
because of their aromatic seeds, it would be
senseless to attack them with a sledgehammer. Nor would
a wise farmer use some kind of rolling device to extract
seeds, for they would be crushed and rendered useless.
Furthermore, herbs grow in small quantities, so hand flail-
ing is practical.

This passage of Scripture goes on to show that
there is a purpose in all this work. The farmer is looking
ahead. Grain has to be ground to make bread for his family. Unlike animals, people have a sense of the future. They
can plan and work toward a goal.

Today, when animal rights activists are trying to
blur the distinction between panthers and people, we need
to be reminded that God has endowed us with special abil-
ities. We do not operate merely on instinct to preserve our
species. We use knowledge and experience.

But neither are we to become totally self-centered,
thinking that we human beings are the center of the

universe and masters of our fate. All of our wisdom comes from God, who graciously shares some of it with us. He gives us counsel. He does not keep all he knows to himself, leaving us to flounder and fail in our attempts to live from day to day.

As we have learned how to pull a carrot out of the ground, but gently pluck a tomato from its vine, we can reflect on God's gift of wisdom for even the most basic of tasks.

HEARTICULTURE: How many times have you had to figure out something all by yourself? There was no precedent for the experience. You had no directions. God simply showed you what to do. Did you thank him?

HORTICULTURE: Most herbs need a sunny location. The oils which account for the herb's flavor are produced in the greatest quantity when plants receive six to eight hours of full sunlight every day. Many herbs will tolerate light shade, but their growth and quality will not be as good.

Water Power

They will come and shout for joy on the heights of Zion; they will rejoice in the bounty of the LORD—the grain, the new wine and the oil, the young of the flocks and herds. They will be like a well-watered garden, and they will sorrow no more.

—JEREMIAH 31:12

The newest home improvement phenomenon in our neighborhood is the installation of underground watering systems. Sprayers are strategically placed in the front yard to shoot water on the lawn and flower beds. Some of these have automatic timers and perform their function even while it is raining!

I am increasingly impressed by the power of water. I may have healthy plants and good soil, but it is regular watering that makes the difference. Annuals, purchased in flats, have such tiny root systems that two days of dry soil does them in. Shrubs that suffer through a fall drought, if not thoroughly watered before winter sets in, will succumb to all sorts of maladies the following spring.

A well-watered garden, bursting with vegetables and grains, is a description of Israel when the Lord returns his people to their own land. Jeremiah prophesied that there will be such abundance that young and old will dance and be glad. Looking beyond the immediate future, God promises a new covenant, or agreement, with his people when he puts his law in their minds and hearts. He will be their God and they will be his people.

This promise was fulfilled in Jesus Christ. He is the Water of Life that nourishes and strengthens us.

HEARTICULTURE: Jesus described himself as "a spring of water welling up to eternal life" (John 4:14). This is a never-ceasing, never-stagnating body of water, which will continue until we come to perfection, eternal life at last. In the person of the Holy Spirit, this spring resides in those who know Jesus as Savior and Lord.

HORTICULTURE: Flowers and vegetables need moisture on their roots, but may suffer from wet leaves, which can encourage the growth of plant disease organisms. A soaker hose is ideal here. Permanent irrigation systems, with coupling devices for expansion, are worth considering for a large garden.

Whither the Willow?

He took some of the seed of your land and put it in fertile soil. He planted it like a willow by abundant water, and it sprouted and became a low, spreading vine. Its branches turned toward him, but its roots remained under it. So it became a vine and produced branches and put out leafy boughs.

—EZEKIEL 17:5–6

Twenty years ago, when we first moved to our present home, there was a willow tree between our yard and the one on the left. According to neighbors, it was planted there by a former owner, who only planted things she could get "for free."

The tree grew to prodigious size and, true to its nature, developed many dead limbs, which fell to the ground during a storm. Our intention to cut down the willow tree before someone was injured was hastened when our neighbor told us about a major problem he had had with water backing up in his basement. The repair man's investigation had revealed the roots of our willow tree reaching out to encircle the underground plumbing! A tree surgeon was called, and the tree was removed.

A willow will always seek water. It was designed by its Creator to grow beside "abundant water," a pond or stream. That's why it's not a good choice for planting in a suburban yard.

From time to time in our lives, we find ourselves with a "willow tree"—a perfectly good thing in itself, but completely out of place. A hobby, a sport, or some other activity which started out as quite harmless, becomes a priority, consuming more and more of our time. It may even become dangerous to our health or well-being or jeopardize our relationships with other people. But we keep putting off the necessary surgery until someone else, possibly a person who is not a Christian, points out the danger.

Pruning of our extracurricular activities may be all that is needed, but if their roots are very deep, only complete removal will be effective.

HEARTICULTURE: In Matthew 6:21 we read, "For where your treasure is, there your heart will be also." It is very easy to ascertain what is most important to you. Just ask yourself: On what do I spend most of my money? Where do I we spend most of my time? Is there an activity that is overwhelming me? Even gardening?

HORTICULTURE: Beware of fast-growing trees such as willows, poplars, and silver maples. They are not very strong, tend to break during storms, and in many cases die young. An oak tree takes longer to grow, but improves with age—like fruitcakes and violins.

The Peaceful Fig Tree

*In the last days. . . . Every man will sit under his
own vine and under his own fig tree, and no one
will make them afraid, for the LORD Almighty
has spoken. All the nations may walk in the
name of their gods; we will walk in the name of
the LORD our God for ever and ever.*
                                        —MICAH 4:1, 4–5

From Genesis through Revelation, depending
upon the translation, we find mention of the fig
tree forty-seven to sixty times. The fig was a symbol of
peace and prosperity, and its possession was the goal of
every Hebrew home owner. The fruit, either fresh or
dried, was highly prized. And the man who owned a fig
tree large enough to sit under was blessed indeed.

We may own something valuable, yet never have
time to enjoy it. My husband and I took a walk the other
evening and marveled at a couple who were peacefully sitting on their deck. Most of the time we are far too busy to
relax in the very setting we've designed for that purpose.

Here the prophet Micah describes the atmosphere
in which *every* person will dwell someday—prosperity without fear. This idyllic age is related to the coming of Jesus
Christ. It is Jesus who makes all the difference. He who is
the Prince of Peace plants in the heart of every believer the
assurance of God's peace, even in the midst of fightings
and fears.

Ours is an imperfect age, but we can still enjoy a measure of the peace that passes understanding, with the promise of perfect peace in the life to come.

HEARTICULTURE: The announcement of the Savior's birth was a proclamation of peace (Luke 2:14). The first thing Jesus said to the disciples when he appeared to them after his resurrection was, "Peace be with you!" (John 20:19). This peace comes only with the indwelling of the Holy Spirit. Is he controlling your life?

HORTICULTURE: The fig tree described here is not the ubiquitous ficus that adorns the atrium in every office building. That is *ficus recusa nitida*. If you want to grow an edible fig tree, buy *ficus carica*. This tree can grow, and possibly even produce figs, in a tub. Provide filtered light, even moisture, heavy soil with good drainage, well-circulating dry air, and cool night temperatures. In southern states fig trees can be grown outside.

When Your Garden Does Not Grow

*Though the fig tree does not bud and there are
no grapes on the vines, though the olive crop
fails and the fields produce no food, though there
are no sheep in the pen and no cattle in the
stalls, yet I will rejoice in the LORD, I will be joyful in God my Savior. The Sovereign LORD is my
strength; he makes my feet like the feet of a deer,
he enables me to go on the heights.*
— HABAKKUK 3:17–19

Every gardener knows what disappointment is. There are some years when the weather is adverse, the animals and insects voracious. (A friend of mine lost his entire tomato crop to a hungry deer who confidently invaded his suburban neighborhood.) So we feel sorry for ourselves and buy what we need from the supermarket. Next year will be better, we hope.

But for those who lived in Habakkuk's day, there was no other source of food. If the olive crop failed, there were no olives. Few sheep in the pen one year meant fewer sheep in the pen next year. In a land where milk and honey flowed, there was sometimes poverty and destitution.

How could Habakkuk be joyful when his crops failed? Because his eyes were fixed, not on the soil, but on the Sovereign Lord. Habakkuk was sure of his personal salvation for today and Jehovah's provision for tomorrow.

This was the source of the prophet's strength. His trembling, faltering feet became as swift and as sure as a deer, able to climb the high hills of adversity.

Habakkuk spoke not only for himself, but also for his people. As a member of the Church of God, to which he belonged through his faith in the Redeemer-Savior, he was sure of final triumph over its enemies.

Yes, sometimes a garden fails. So may a marriage, a friendship, or a business association. A beloved child rebels. Our church experiences dissension. A relationship we have carefully nurtured for years bears no fruit and dries up.

We need not despair. Our Sovereign Lord offers us his strength, even his joy, to go on to victory.

HEARTICULTURE: David was well acquainted with failure. In Psalm 28 he says, "The LORD is my strength and my shield; my heart trusts in him, and I am helped. My heart leaps for joy and I will give thanks to him in song" (v. 7). Look beyond your present disappointment to God's promise of continuing support.

HORTICULTURE: A garden journal is an invaluable help in determining the causes of our successes and failures. This record need not be elaborate. But a few notes about new seeds and plants we have tried, the demise of an old favorite, what happened when we transplanted, and how our environment has changed over the years, will guide us when we plot out our garden for the coming year. While spring flowering bulbs are still in bloom, it is helpful to sketch their placement in the garden, especially if we overplant the beds with annuals.

Lilies Aren't Lilies

And why do you worry about clothes? See how the lilies of the field grow. They do not labor or spin. Yet I tell you that not even Solomon in all his splendor was dressed like one of these.
—MATTHEW 6:28–29

Picture Jesus standing on a hillside among a sea of flowers. Picking one, he holds it up while he speaks of this passage to the crowd. Tradition has decreed that the "lily" be a *longiflorum*, an Easter lily, forced to bloom in time for that one special day. This is a precarious undertaking for a greenhouse. No one wants an Easter lily in full bloom three days before Easter, and fabulous blossoms that appear the day after have no market value whatsoever.

Jesus was not looking out over a meadow of *longiflori*. The flowers could have been anemones, asphodelines, field daisies, tulips, even field flowers such as alfalfa or timothy. One expert on biblical agriculture reasons that whatever flower it was, its blossom was large enough to be seen from a distance.

Jesus used as his example a wildflower. While it can be said that the *liliflorum* itself does not toil, it certainly requires a lot of work on the part of the employees in the greenhouse! The wildflower, however, grows without tending. During the fleeting Palestinian spring, hundreds of varieties of flowers spring up to signal nature's awakening.

The point of Jesus' visual aid is not to decry industry. We are not instructed to sit still and expect God to provide for us. Jesus is telling us not to worry so much about what we will wear that we forget to seek what is really important—his kingdom and his righteousness. In fact, if we make these our primary concerns, God promises to provide everything else we need.

HEARTICULTURE: If we truly seek God's kingdom and his righteousness, our assessment of our needs will change. The basics of food and clothing which Jesus discusses here will preclude many of the luxuries which we formerly classified as necessities.

HORTICULTURE: When the last blooms of your Easter lily have faded, cut them off, remove the plant with dirt intact from its pot, and sink it into a sunny spot in your garden. The following year it will bloom at the appointed time for lilies.

Bumper Crop

*A farmer went out to sow his seed. As he was
scattering the seed, some fell along the path, and
the birds came and ate it up. Some fell on rocky
places, where it did not have much soil. It sprang
up quickly, because the soil was shallow. But
when the sun came up, the plants were scorched,
and they withered because they had no root.
Other seed fell among thorns, which grew up and
choked the plants. Still other seed fell on good
soil, where it produced a crop—a hundred, sixty
or thirty times what was sown. He who has ears,
let him hear.*

—MATTHEW 13:3–9

This biblical parable is, truly, the gardener's
promise! Everything that happened to that
farmer I have also experienced. Birds have eaten my seed.
Zinnias have sprung up and then suddenly died. I found a
slab of rock four inches below the ground. Thorns have
taken over a plot of asters. Ah, but then I think about all
the good soil that bore flowers and vegetables far beyond
my expectations.

Beginning with verse 18 in this chapter, Jesus carefully explains the parable's meaning. The sower is Jesus
Christ who proclaims a message about himself and his
kingdom. The soil is the condition of our hearts. Some
people hear the message and refuse to find out what it
means. Some hear it with enthusiasm, but can't stand up to

persecution when it comes. Others receive the Word until worries and the deceitfulness of wealth (already planted, but not evident) choke it out. Finally, there is the one who hears the Word and understands it. He produces a good crop—the fruit of the Holy Spirit as defined in Galatians 5:22–23.

Note that there is never anything deficient about the seed. There have always been those who would change the message, add to it or leave some of it out, hybridize it perhaps, or mix it with other seed. But it is only the message proclaimed by Jesus Christ that produces the good crop, even in the good soil.

Those of us who spend hours poring over seed catalogs to select exactly the right seeds, should surely be as careful to seek the truth of God's Word as it appears in the Scriptures. No flower or vegetable can be better than the seed that produces it.

HEARTICULTURE: The rate of return on this seed varies, but even thirtyfold is a creditable increase. As in other parables, Jesus does not condemn the heart that produces less, nor praise the heart that produces more. He recognizes that even among good soils there are different capacities. What matters is that one produce a crop.

HORTICULTURE: A general rule for planting seeds is to plant twice as many as you think you will need. Gauge the depth of planting by the size of the seed. The tiniest seeds need no covering at all.

Seeds or Weeds?

Jesus told them another parable: "The kingdom of heaven is like a man who sowed good seed in his field. But while everyone was sleeping, his enemy came and sowed weeds among the wheat, and went away. When the wheat sprouted and formed heads, then the weeds also appeared."

The owner's servants came to him and said, "Sir, didn't you sow good seed in your field? Where then did the weeds come from?"

"An enemy did this," he replied.

The servants asked him, "Do you want us to go and pull them up?"

"No," he answered, "because while you are pulling the weeds, you may root up the wheat with them. Let both grow together until the harvest. At that time I will tell the harvesters: First collect the weeds and tie them in bundles to be burned, then gather the wheat and bring it into my barn."

—*MATTHEW 13:24–30*

Jesus certainly had a lot to say about weeds! In this curious story, an enemy comes into the wheat fields at night and sows weeds. But the farmer doesn't even seem disturbed. We will understand why if we look at his reaction from the Middle Eastern point of view, where the pace of life is slower, and people are more resigned to the inevitable setbacks of life.

Whereas we would rush out and cover the fields with a selective herbicide, the Palestinian farmer bides his time, knowing the weeds can be routed out when the crop is mature. And this is the point of the parable: There are real Christians and pretend Christians, and the difference between them is very hard to distinguish.

When we hear that someone has come to know the Lord, we wonder if the conversion was "genuine." Or church members may act inconsistently, and the question arises as to whether they were really saved in the first place. Jesus tells us that only God knows for sure. Therefore, while we need to be discerning in our relationships—and the Scriptures give us many guidelines for ascertaining our own spiritual state and the spiritual state of others—the final judgment will be made by God. We are to be patient and leave the matter up to him.

In this parable there is a less obvious but nevertheless important truth for the "wheaty Christians." God will judge us fairly, too! We may struggle and fall back, sin, repent, and sin again, but if our love for the Lord is real, at harvest time we shall be brought into the heavenly barn.

HEARTICULTURE: The second and third chapters of Colossians are worth serious, repeated study as we seek to understand our own spiritual state and determine, in a limited way, the genuineness of another's commitment to Christ.

HORTICULTURE: I always appreciate it when a seed packet includes a picture of the baby seedling. I once carefully cultivated a whole row of purslane! When you know what a true seedling looks like, make a little sketch for future reference. It also helps to know what the weeds look like!

Pruning Is Painful

Early in the morning, as he was on his way back to the city, he [Jesus] was hungry. Seeing a fig tree by the road, he went up to it but found nothing on it except leaves. Then he said to it, "May you never bear fruit again!" Immediately the tree withered.

—*MATTHEW 21:18–19*

A peculiarity of the fig tree is that the fruit and leaves usually appear at the same time, with the fruit sometimes coming first. In this passage, it is late spring, and the tree has put forth leaves but has produced no fruit. Jesus is not punishing this tree for failing to bear fruit, but is using the tree—a common fig symbolizing the nation of Israel—as a graphic illustration of his chosen people's unfruitfulness.

When you have a fruit tree that doesn't bear fruit, what do you do? In Luke 13:6–9, Jesus told the story of a man with this problem. The owner of a vineyard had waited three years but when his fig tree didn't produce in all that time, he ordered the man who tended his vineyard to cut the tree down. The caretaker asked the owner to wait one more year, so he could dig around it and fertilize it. Maybe the tree could yet be encouraged to produce fruit.

God is patient and merciful, but he is also just. He may wait another year for those who have heard his Word to respond to it, but there comes a time when he will wait no longer. If we, like the fig tree, cannot be prodded into fruit-bearing, as evidence of our love for Jesus Christ, we will be destroyed. This a harsh word, but God created us, and he has the right to make such a drastic decision.

HEARTICULTURE: If you were a fig tree, would the Master be disappointed in your fruit? Do you need some fertilizer from God's Word, or a few sharp digs in your surroundings? Pruning is painful but is often the only growth stimulus that works.

HORTICULTURE: Unproductive mature fruit trees can be reinvigorated by dormant-season and summer pruning. Follow specific directions in a reliable garden guide. Up to one-half of the total wood can be removed from peaches or Japanese plums, one-third of the wood of apples, cherries, apricots, or European plums. Pears are more fragile and can suffer loss from one-tenth of their total wood.

Nine Mint Leaves for Me

Woe to you, teachers of the law and Pharisees,
you hypocrites! You give a tenth of your spices—
mint, dill and cummin. But you have neglected
the more important matters of the law—justice,
mercy and faithfulness. You should have prac-
ticed the latter, without neglecting the former.
You blind guides! You strain out a gnat but
swallow a camel.

—MATTHEW 23:23–24

In catalogs and in garden centers, herbs are always pictured as cute little potted plants that can supposedly be grown on your windowsill. Actually, most herbs develop into huge bushes or spread out all over the place, defying eradication. Mint, with its underground trailing suckers, is a rampant grower that you will have with you forever.

Giving a tenth, a *tithe*, of one's mint meant stripping off all the leaves and counting them by tens—nine for me, one for the Lord, nine for me, one for the Lord. What a tedious business that must have been. It was, however, a measurable task that would produce a feeling of great accomplishment. You wouldn't give the Lord too much, but you wouldn't shortchange him, either.

On the other hand, justice, mercy, and faithfulness can't be measured. When is a Christian faithful *enough*? This kind of spiritual practice just keeps on expanding, as the Lord intended. Furthermore, *being* is not as obvious as *doing.* Every church is familiar with the "anonymous donor" who gives the sanctuary piano or the office computer, but being merciful doesn't even rate a mention in the church bulletin.

Tithing is a biblical practice the Lord promises to bless. In obedience to him, we are to give a minimum of one-tenth of our income. Our material wealth, however, can never be a substitute for a compassionate heart. It is our being, not our doing, to which the Lord assigns the greater value.

HEARTICULTURE: Jesus was not telling the Pharisees something new. The prophet Micah wrote, "And what does the LORD require of you? To act justly and to love mercy and to walk humbly with your God" (6:8). God has never been pleased with offerings that proceed from sinful motives.

HORTICULTURE: Mint can be controlled by growing it in a pot or in a bottomless bucket sunk in the soil. It likes to be cool, damp, and shaded, but it is very adaptable. It is an excellent plant to secure soil on a slope—which should tell you something.

A Place of Prayer

*Then Jesus went with his disciples to a place
called Gethsemane, and he said to them, "Sit here
while I go over there and pray." He took Peter
and the two sons of Zebedee along with him, and
he began to be sorrowful and troubled. Then he
said to them, "My soul is overwhelmed with sorrow to the point of death. Stay here and keep
watch with me."*

—*MATTHEW 26:36–38*

Gardeners love to visit gardens. We tour gardens in China or New Zealand, drop by the
Butchart Gardens in Victoria on a trip to Canada, and fly to
England just to attend the Chelsea Flower Show. Traveling
through our own United States, we always look for a garden
to enjoy. We even arrange tours of gardens in our garden
club!

Whether Gethsemane was a formally designed garden with flower beds or simply an olive grove, we do not
know. The name itself means "oil press," so we do know
that olive trees grew there and still do. But we also know
that it was a favorite retreat frequented by Jesus and his disciples, a most suitable place for prayer.

In contrast to the Garden of Eden, where the first
Adam succumbed to temptation, the second Adam over-
came it in the Garden of Gethsemane. Falling with his face
to the ground (an uncharacteristic posture for prayer),
Jesus accepted his Father's will that he should go to the
cross. In this time of agony he was in every way as human

as divine, anticipating the incomparable pain that was to follow.

There are two principle ways to resist temptation— watch and pray. Exhausted "from sorrow," John says, the disciples could do neither. They had reached that need for sleep which forces the eyes to close no matter how hard one tries to resist. In this vulnerable state, his friends were unable to support Jesus during his time of humiliation and suffering.

A garden causes us to reflect on all the attributes of God. We see his creative and sustaining power, his sovereignty, his infinity and majesty. Whether we tend a border of flowers or a half-acre of vegetables, a garden reminds us of our dependence on God. As we see evidence of our own imperfections, we remember that garden in Gethsemane, long ago, where our Savior said, "My Father . . . may your will be done" (Matt. 26:42).

HEARTICULTURE: All four gospels describe events that took place in the Garden of Gethsemane. Do we see its importance in God's plan for our redemption? As you view a garden, reflect on it as a symbol of God's love for you.

HORTICULTURE: Gardeners usually spend so much time keeping their plants in order that they often don't take time to sit back and enjoy them. Consider a place of meditation in your landscaping plan. A lounge chair in a shady spot or a bench under a tree can draw us aside to rest and pray.

Know Your Weeds

Still others, like seed sown among thorns, hear the word; but the worries of this life, the deceitfulness of wealth and the desires for other things come in and choke the word, making it unfruitful.

—MARK 4:18–19

LaVerne and I went down to the entrance of our subdivision and attacked the pernicious grass that grows into the shrubs and flowers framing our brick sign. The tendrils of this weed often stretch three feet or more, spreading underground with a tenacity that makes weeding almost impossible. They will just as easily grow over the top, killing whatever is underneath.

We can, with much effort, pull the weed up, but we know it will grow back as soon as we leave it unattended. We also know that the tiniest section left in the ground will sprout with unusual vigor. As I knelt there, ripping out these tenacious tendrils, I thought of how much they resemble "the worries of this life, the deceitfulness of wealth and the desires for other things" which come in and choke the teachings of God's Word.

Worry, deceitfulness, and unholy desires have to be torn out of our hearts. But we can't do that job one time and then put away our trowels. No, we have to keep watching for those weeds to spring up again, then battle them at their source. While eradication is impossible, control is entirely realistic if we are vigilant.

It is God's Word that provides our defense against sinful appetites, and this is what Jesus is talking about here. A brief Sunday morning shot will not do as much good as a daily immersion. As with all weeding, the best results come from surveying our ground often, identifying the invader, and responding with the most effective method. Dandelions and crabgrass are not treated in the same way. God's Word also offers specific help for specific problems. Use your Bible as a practical manual for attacking problems in your life.

HEARTICULTURE: Do we view deceit and unworthy desires as harmful to our spiritual health as weeds are to our garden? Are we as persistent in their eradication? The word *choke* infers strength, determination, and the desire to kill. Only God's Word is powerful enough to save us from such an experience!

HORTICULTURE: I once regarded a study of weeds as a waste of time. I didn't need to know what they *were*, I thought. I just needed to know what they *weren't*! Then I found out that weeds can be dicots, monocots, annuals, biennials, and perennials, and that there are different ways to control each type. *When* I applied the weed killer was as important as what I used. Today there are hundreds of specific chemicals, as well as organic soaps and sprays for that purpose. Learning about weeds is time (and money!) well spent.

Sowing the Seed

This is what the kingdom of God is like. A man scatters seed on the ground. Night and day, whether he sleeps or gets up, the seed sprouts and grows, though he does not know how. All by itself the soil produces grain—first the stalk, then the head, then the full kernel in the head. As soon as the grain is ripe, he puts the sickle to it, because the harvest has come.

—MARK 4:26–29

A careful study of the flowers contained in a wildflower seed mixture or pictured in a wildflower guide, reveals the surprising fact that we are seeing the same perennials we buy as plants in a gardening center. While we fertilize our oriental poppies, adding some manure for extra help, this same species grows in great drifts on some hillside. We dig in manure around our asters, too, and water them regularly, yet they bloom in profusion in almost every meadow.

Obviously, plants, especially grains, can grow without human assistance. I have had some great flowers planted by birds! So it is with the kingdom of God. As important as personal witnessing is, there *are* people who come into the kingdom without any cultivation at all. They may read a Gideon Bible in a hotel room, or hear a radio program, or decide to attend church, even without an invitation, and there they accept Jesus as their Lord and Savior. I have a friend who was saved after seeing the movie, "Quo Vadis."

Jesus reminds us in this parable that if the soil—the heart—is prepared to accept the seed—the Word—the Word will take root and grow. God seeks out and saves those whom he will, and nothing can impede his grace. This truth does not excuse us from sharing the gospel, however, for God has ordained us as his witnesses. Still, we are to remember that the seed is more essential than the way in which it is sown.

HEARTICULTURE: The major blessing in reading or hearing personal testimonies of salvation is the realization that God works in so many creative ways to build his kingdom. Paul's well-known thoughts on this subject are worth rereading. (See 1 Corinthians 9:19–23.)

HORTICULTURE: Probably the least interesting and most tedious aspect of gardening is preparing the soil. We must begin with a soil analysis, usually through our county cooperative extension service, and go on from there to add recommended supplements, to till, to remove rocks, to rake, and finally to plant the seed. Then begins the lifelong process of adding compost, weeding, rotating crops, and adding nutrients again. It is foolish to put an expensive plant in poor soil, whereas even a mediocre plant can thrive in good soil.

117

More Than a Tithe

*Woe to you Pharisees, because you give God a
tenth of your mint, rue and all other kinds of
garden herbs, but you neglect justice and the love
of God. You should have practiced the latter
without leaving the former undone.*

—LUKE 11:42

Since Jesus spoke these words prior to eating
dinner, he could have been reminded of rue,
since it was often used as a flavoring for food as well as
medicine. What started the whole discourse was the host
Pharisee's surprise that Jesus did not first wash before he
ate, a ritual required by ceremonial law. Jesus took the
opportunity to point out that Pharisees paid much attention to outward appearances and very little attention to the
condition of their hearts.

From other accounts we have of the Pharisees, we
can surmise that when they gave their carefully counted
herb leaves, they didn't just slip them in through the back
door of the temple. Such donations were accompanied by
a carefully staged drama to impress onlookers.

Jesus did not condemn the Pharisees for their
practice of tithing. He knew that it took funds to maintain
God's temple, and it still does. Jesus' rebuke was leveled at
the belief that supporting the church financially can be a
substitute for actual ministry on its behalf.

As we care for the poor, we will be burdened to give
beyond the basic ten percent. Personal involvement shows

us how much we have and how little we really have given. "Practicing" justice means more than sending in a check. It means hands-on participation in the lives of others—repairing a broken window or taking a sick child to a clinic—and it does what money cannot immediately do.

The foundation of such a living faith is our love of God. This springs out of a humble, obedient heart responding to God's love for us in the sacrifice of his only Son.

HEARTICULTURE: What does God ask of his people? In Deuteronomy 10:12–13, we learn the answer. "And now, O Israel, what does the LORD your God ask of you but to fear the LORD your God, to walk in all his ways, to love him, to serve the LORD your God with all your heart and with all your soul, and to observe the LORD's commands and decrees that I am giving you today for your own good?"

HORTICULTURE: The herb rue can grow to a height of three feet. In the fall it should be pruned back to the old wood. Rue is a hardy, tolerant plant which provides an attractive background for lower-growing flowers. But beware! It is pungent and can be toxic to the skin.

A Kernel of Wheat

*I tell you the truth, unless a kernel of wheat falls
to the ground and dies, it remains only a single
seed. But if it dies, it produces many seeds. The
man who loves his life will lose it, while the man
who hates his life in this world will keep it for
eternal life.*

—*JOHN 12:24–25*

Jesus was the master in illustrating spiritual
truth. After hearing this example of the wheat
kernel, all his disciples must have nodded their heads and
said, "Of course! A seed won't produce more seeds unless
it is planted!" Even fishermen and tax collectors knew that
much about farming.

Jesus was, first of all, talking about himself. He had
to humiliate himself, descend from heaven to earth, and
be crucified to accomplish our redemption. He lay in the
ground, under the clods of earth, to spring forth fresh and
alive. And there was a great increase—one dying Christ
produced thousands of living Christians.

There is also a lesson for us. Each of us is a seed,
figuratively speaking, stored in a cool, dry place—a secure
little world where we are totally safe. We may delude ourselves into thinking we have real happiness, even though
we may never have ventured forth to discover anything
else.

Like Jesus, we have to break out of our confine-
ment, fall to the ground where we are trampled on, be

subjected to the rigors of changing temperatures and humidity, and suffer attacks by an army of pests and diseases, before we can survive and produce a host of new seeds. What is even more incredible is Jesus' assurance that in this process we shall discover true happiness!

Jesus defines this happiness as being honored by the Father. We shall experience his presence in this life and then enjoy his presence in heaven forevermore.

HEARTICULTURE: "See here the fatal consequences of an inordinate love of life; many a man hugs himself to death, and loses his life by overloving it. He that so loves his animal life shall thereby shorten his days, shall lose the life he is so fond of, and another infinitely better."
Matthew Henry

HORTICULTURE: In the spring, gift catalogs advertise Easter baskets containing a growing medium that will produce "real grass." The seeds are actually wheat seeds, which can be purchased inexpensively and then sown in a basket lined with plastic and filled with a potting mixture.

The Gardener's Voice

They [two angels] asked her, "Woman, why are
you crying?" "They have taken my Lord away,"
she said, "and I don't know where they have put
him." At this, she turned around and saw Jesus
standing there, but she did not realize that it was
Jesus. "Woman," he said, "why are you crying?
Who is it you are looking for?" Thinking he was
the gardener, she said, "Sir, if you have carried
him away, tell me where you have put him, and I
will get him." Jesus said to her, "Mary." She
turned toward him and cried out in Aramaic,
"Rabboni!" (which means Teacher).
—JOHN 20:13–16

In his account of Jesus' death and burial, John described the place where his tomb was located as a garden. Evidence of first-century tombs, hewn from walls of rock, supports the fact that they were not always in a location conducive to plants and trees. But Nicodemus's new tomb was in a garden, and it was there that Jesus' body, wrapped in linen, was laid.

This garden must have been unusually fine, for Mary Magdalene presumed that it had a gardener and that he would be the logical person to ask about the removal of her Lord. Jesus' glorified body was so like and yet so unlike that which she had known, that she did not recognize him at first.

Mary could not mistake the voice, however, especially when he spoke her name. We also often fail to recognize the Lord when he comes to us "in a different form," but we cannot fail to recognize him when he speaks our name. When we truly love someone and are loved in return, the ear can discern what the eye fails to distinguish. When we stand at the bedside of a relative who is seriously ill, our first words are that person's name, and it is their response, however feeble, that offers hope.

As you stand in your "garden" today, what is Jesus saying to you?

HEARTICULTURE: We read in John 10:4 that Jesus' sheep know his voice. Whatever your burden or distress, you have only to call out to him, and he will speak to you through his Word.

HORTICULTURE: To perpetuate the memory of a loved one, you might take a cutting from a favorite plant or grow a flower that reminds you of that person. If your church property is suitable, perhaps you could get permission to plant a meditation garden in his or her memory, complete with a bench. Keep the setting simple and easy to maintain.

From Death to Life

*What you sow does not come to life unless it dies.
When you sow, you do not plant the body that
will be, but just a seed, perhaps of wheat or of
something else. But God gives it a body as he has
determined, and to each kind of seed he gives its
own body.*

—*1 Corinthians 15:36–38*

Cut a bulb in half, and you will see the entire plant, flower and all, neatly tucked inside. This is not true of a seed. Once, before planting morning glories, I deliberately nicked each seed with a knife. The ones I cut in half by mistake did not contain a flowering vine, ready to uncoil and wrap itself around my mailbox post.

Whatever may be the botanical explanation, something extraordinary happens to a seed after it is planted. God gives each seed its proper body as he has determined. Do you not marvel that one tomato seed can produce a plant four feet tall, loaded with red fruit?

When we die, our bodies are sown in the ground. God raises them as spiritual bodies, each one distinct, representative of its previous owner and yet bearing Christ's likeness. This is a truth that is hard for us to grasp, and yet it is no more difficult for God to raise a spiritual body from a physical body than it is for him to raise a plant from a seed.

Knowing that our grave is not the end of life, but simply God's way of planting us so that we can be resurrected, makes that event one of expectation rather than of fear and dread. Because Christ rose from the dead, we who believe in him shall rise from the dead also. Thanks be to God who gives us the victory!

HEARTICULTURE: Paul is always realistic. In 2 Corinthians 4:16–18, he admits that even though outwardly we are wasting away (getting older), we are being renewed inwardly day by day (growing more like Christ). Christ is the unseen reality on which we fix our eyes.

HORTICULTURE: While seed tapes are more expensive than seed packets, there are some advantages to the tapes: Thinning is not necessary, and you can place the seeds exactly where you want them, without transplanting tender plants later on. On the market now are seed "carpets"— pressed soil imbedded with seeds. The carpet can be cut into any shape to fit a container or left in the roll to plant as a unit.

Spiritual Fruit

But the fruit of the Spirit is love, joy, peace, patience, kindness, goodness, faithfulness, gentleness and self-control. Against such things there is no law.

—GALATIANS 5:22

When I first heard about the fruit of the Spirit, I thought of a bowl with nine different kinds of fruit in it. As I grew in my faith, I felt I might be a loving pear and a kind nectarine, but bypass entirely the self-controlled pineapple.

Our women's group recently did a Bible study with visual aids, and I was absolutely amazed to discover that the fruit of the Spirit was represented by a single bunch of grapes. Furthermore, I learned that the Bible doesn't use the word *fruits*, but *fruit*—it is all one thing! If one has the fruit of the Spirit, one has nine different virtues—in differing measure, perhaps, but all are present. The Holy Spirit does not give us the right to make a personal selection. So I can't say, "I've never been patient, but that's just the way I am."

In our group we spent nine weeks studying each of the nine virtues, which was only a start, of course, for there is no end to the richness of the fruit of the Holy Spirit. We all learned to recite the virtues, being careful to include the little phrase at the end, "Against such things there is no law."

What does that mean? Law means restraint. There are no restrictions or limits on the fruit of the Spirit. These virtues are the result of God's grace, and as such, are boundless. We are free to enjoy them all!

HEARTICULTURE: Jesus tells us in John 15:16 that he chose us to go and bear fruit—fruit that will last. This is not a suggestion, but a mandate.

HORTICULTURE: If fruit trees and grapes are not your type of gardening, how about strawberries? In the expectation that one plant plus its daughter plants will produce one quart of berries, twenty-five to fifty plants will provide adequately for a family of four. Space plants thirty to thirty-six inches apart in rows forty-two to forty-eight inches apart.

Sowing and Reaping

*Do not be deceived: God cannot be mocked. A
man reaps what he sows.*

—GALATIANS 6:7

For anyone having even a modicum of interest in gardening, the truth of this passage is so
obvious as to be undeserving of further attention. Of
course, we get *out of* the ground what we put *into* the
ground! If I plant one row of carrots, I will not reap ten
rows of carrots or one row of nasturtiums.

But there is another point that is not quite so obvious—the idea that God cannot be mocked. Unfortunately,
there resides within human nature the notion that we can
get away with a sin or two, especially if they are "little"
sins. Even those who commit adultery or embezzlement do
not expect to be caught—by God or anyone else!

But these words are for Christians, church members. Paul, who wrote them, did not limit his concern to
actions judged wrong by society's liberal standards. He
warned us to watch ourselves in the basic sin of pride. If
we do good only to please ourselves, we will reap destruction. Paul is quite blunt about that!

One of the most curious aspects of gardening is
how a seed sown the previous year will sprout up in spite
of tilling, spading, mulching, or over-seeding. Tomatoes
have this habit. They serve as a visual reminder that our
sowing may remain hidden for a time, but the evidence
will eventually appear.

HEARTICULTURE: How long can we get away with something? Read about the final harvest in Revelation 14:14–16.

HORTICULTURE: When sowing seeds under lights, use indelible ink on your identification markers. I planted six colors of peppers last winter, but the ink on my paper markers washed off under the spray. When I wanted to select two plants from each color, I couldn't tell one from the other. All the plants looked the same, of course. Do identify every set of plants. As the trays are rotated under the lights, it is very easy to lose track.

Abundant Harvest

The one who sows to please his sinful nature,
from that nature will reap destruction; the one
who sows to please the Spirit, from the Spirit will
reap eternal life. Let us not become weary in
doing good, for at the proper time we will reap a
harvest if we do not give up.

—GALATIANS 6:8–9

Who will be the first to pick a ripe tomato? The person who bought a mature tomato plant already laden with green fruit has a decided jump on the person who started plants from seed and had to wait an extra week to set them out due to cold weather. Tomatoes have a way of catching up, however. One set of seedlings I put out this spring were yellow, rootbound, and decidedly puny. But by midsummer, they were as vigorous as plants I have purchased. It is the harvest that counts.

We might say that the real question should be, "Who will be the *last* to pick a ripe tomato?" Another good question is, "Who will pick the most tomatoes?" My first patio tomato plant bore two fruit.

What is the Christian's harvest? Souls, of course. Many of these take a very long time to blossom and require patient cultivation. Mature believers are a worthy crop, but faithful tending of young spirits is necessary, too.

We are not to become weary. In spite of drought, floods, erosion, clay, sand, rocks, weeds, rabbits, dogs, cats, raccoons, gophers, mice, moles, squirrels, deer (in Alaska a friend had problems with a moose!), rocks, weeds, thorns, birds, insects, diseases, fungi, children, frost, heat, cold, and the tool we loaned out and didn't get back, we are not to become weary! If we sow to please the Spirit, we shall reap to please the Spirit. God will enable us to overcome. Hallelujah!

HEARTICULTURE: Notice that in this passage God does not say, "Do not grow *tired*." *Tired* is different from *weary*, which implies both physical and mental exhaustion. *Weary* also involves an attitude, a suspicion that the labor was ineffectual or unappreciated. God recognizes hard work. Read Revelation 2:1–3.

HORTICULTURE: As much as we want to get out in the garden, there are times when we must resist the urge. Senior citizens should not work during a heat alert, even in the early evening. Storm warnings should be heeded. And many a back has been injured when a gardener couldn't wait for someone to help lift the railroad tie or the bags of topsoil.

Orchids Take Patience

I thank my God every time I remember you. In all my prayers for all of you, I always pray with joy because of your partnership in the gospel from the first day until now, being confident of this, that he who began a good work in you will carry it on to completion until the day of Christ Jesus.
—PHILIPPIANS 1:3–6

A friend of mine who toured an orchid jungle in Florida was reminded of this verse when she learned that the propagation of orchid plants, by seed or tissue culture, takes years in a carefully controlled environment. To begin the process, a bit of tissue from the plant stem, or seed, is put into a test tube in a sterile nutrient solution. The tube is laid on its side in a wooden rack and agitated gently in monitored conditions of heat and light.

The orchid lover who begins a good work like this has to wait a long time for an orchid. But he doesn't just wait. He has to work, too, checking all the environmental controls, observing the different stages of growth, making necessary changes.

There is tremendous reassurance in the fact that when God begins his work in us, he will carry it through to completion. We get discouraged sometimes, wondering if we are really growing in the Lord. Have we reached a "spiritual plateau," leveled off? But God is not only patient, he is working in us, helping us to change. God is never passive.

The orchid grower is willing to expend so much effort because the result is well worth it—a flower of unsurpassed beauty. God is willing to work in us because the result will be well worth it—"an eternal glory that far outweighs them all" (2 Cor. 4:17). How much God loves us!

HEARTICULTURE: In Colossians 3:10 we read that we have put on a new self which is *being* renewed in knowledge in the image of its Creator. The verb form makes it very clear that our spiritual growth is a process that doesn't end until we arrive in heaven. Thoughtfully examine your own life and note how much change has taken place. Perhaps you weren't even aware of it. Praise God!

HORTICULTURE: Home orchid culture will not result in a corsage for your daughter's prom, but even without a greenhouse you can still grow many kinds of orchids. *Cattleya, laelia, dendrobium, phalaenopsis,* and *paphiopedilum* are varieties that will bloom well on a bright windowsill. Light soil and high humidity are necessary.

The Last Garden

*Then the angel showed me the river of the water
of life, as clear as crystal, flowing from the throne
of God and of the Lamb down the middle of the
great street of the city. On each side of the river
stood the tree of life, bearing twelve crops of fruit,
yielding its fruit every month. And the leaves of
the tree are for the healing of the nations.*
—REVELATION 22:1–2

The Bible ends, as it began, with a garden. This second paradise is free of all evil. There is no serpent. There is no curse, for Christ has removed it, along with its consequences.

The site of paradise (heaven) is dominated by a great tree, so huge it stands on each side of the river of the water of life. This is the ideal tree, for it bears different kinds of fruit all year round. What orchard owner would not covet a tree like that! We can buy apple trees which bear five kinds of apples, but we can't buy apple trees which also bear oranges and peaches, and certainly not every month of the year.

In addition to the fruit, there are healing leaves for the nations, indicating harmony and peace for all peoples. Instead of fighting each other, we shall be serving the Lord together, unhampered by darkness, for that, too, shall be ended.

Another unique aspect of this garden is that it will be enjoyed by all those who belong to the Lord Jesus. The first Paradise, Eden, was inhabited by only two people, but the second paradise shall be inhabited by millions—all the saints saved by the blood of the Lamb. We shall be forever sustained by the life-giving water which flows from God's throne and the delicious fruit of his presence. At last we shall know perfect health and happiness.

This garden is neither a myth nor a vague possibility. It is a reality, assured by our sovereign Lord who has never broken a promise. Jesus invites us to come and take the free gift of the Water of Life. We have only to acknowledge that we are thirsty.

HEARTICULTURE: Long before John had his vision of paradise, the prophet Ezekiel was shown what it would be like. Read about paradise in chapter 47.

HORTICULTURE: Every fruit tree is made of two or more different plants that have been joined together by *grafting*. There is the rootstock, which controls the tree's size and quality, and the bud or stem, which determines the variety. Usually, we select a tree for its variety and never bother to find out whether the rootstock is the most suitable for our area. Unfortunately, this information is seldom available. Buy trees from a company that supplies this information, or ask your local garden center to find out from the wholesale nursery where it purchased the trees.

Prayer
Plants

_____

_____
_____
_____
_____
_____
_____
_____
_____
_____
_____
_____
_____
_____
_____
_____
_____
_____
_____
_____
_____
_____
_____
_____
_____
_____
_____
_____

Prayer
Plants

_____

_____
_____
_____
_____
_____
_____
_____
_____
_____
_____
_____
_____
_____
_____
_____
_____
_____
_____
_____
_____
_____
_____
_____
_____

Prayer Plants

_____

_____
_____
_____
_____
_____
_____
_____
_____
_____
_____
_____
_____
_____
_____
_____
_____
_____
_____
_____
_____
_____
_____
_____
_____

Prayer
Harvest

_____

_____
_____
_____
_____
_____
_____
_____
_____
_____
_____
_____
_____
_____
_____
_____
_____
_____
_____
_____
_____
_____
_____
_____
_____
_____
_____
_____
_____

Prayer
Harvest

Prayer
Harvest